DARK PSYCHOLOGY AND MANIPULATION TECHNIQUES

The Ideal Guide to Understanding the Fundamentals of Manipulation and Mind Control Techniques, Using Psychology to Influence People's Behavior (2022)

Wynne Nelson

CONTENTS

Introduction   5

Chapter 1   6

Chapter 2   10

Chapter 3   17

Chapter 4   32

Chapter 5   48

Chapter 6   65

Chapter 7   88

Conclusion   94

INTRODUCTION

Congratulations on your purchase of Dark Psychology Secrets. I'm impressed that you've accepted the responsibility of learning more about the various types of techniques used for manipulation. This book will provide you with in-depth information about the world of psychology.

You'll quickly discover that there are a lot more details that go into the world of psychology and manipulation. By the end of the day, you should be enlightened about the basics of psychology and their effect in any manipulation scenario.

The information provided here is accurate and provides a realistic impression of psychology. It describes the small terms that are very. You don't have to agonize about the finer details of psychology anymore; they are all described in this awesome document.

Aside from that, the data herein is solely focused on enlightening the readers in the most simple way possible. The words used in this document are easy to understand and are supported by evidence. This eBook will help you understand why it is critical to conduct exclusive research before embarking on a manipulative mission.

Again, there are numerous books on psychology available, but you have chosen this one. Thank you once more for making such a decision. This eBook contains relevant information that you will find extremely useful. Every effort was made to ensure that the document contains accurate information that will not mislead the readers. Thank you once more for devoting your valuable time to downloading this document!

CHAPTER 1
The Art of Manipulation

Manipulation has progressed from simple tricks to more sophisticated ones. Everyone has been manipulated in one way or another without even realizing it. However, a keen analysis reveals that psychology employs huge.

Manipulation is defined as the technique of persuading people to do what you want them to do. It employs the emotional pathway to enter people's minds and persuade them that your way of thinking is the correct one. As a result, they believe that they should blindly follow your ideologies without questioning their authenticity. At the end of the day, the one who has been manipulated frequently does not realize it, especially if the psychologist did a perfect job. At some point, they believe it was their own decision, not realizing that there was a force behind it all. That's why you're often surprised when your favourite psychologist answers one question with another. The idea is to know what you're thinking about and manipulate it so that you feel like the final product is your own decision. If you're not smart enough, you might end up disclosing a lot of information about your relationship. As a result, you'll be highly susceptible to various types of manipulation.

Practising your manipulation skills gives you a good idea of how the whole process works. It is very simple to manipulate a close loved one or friend. Why? Being close to someone allows you to learn about their likes and dislikes. On the plus side, it allows you to analyze what scares them and manipulate them to favour your principles. Manipulation, on the other hand, is an art that, if not done carefully, can jeopardize the relationship of two people. It is therefore extremely important that you study your target before making the final move. Speak with them frequently to obtain detailed information that will be used to manipulate their way of thinking.

When persuading someone, it is critical to make them feel as if the final decision has been their choice all along. You should understand the fundamentals that revolve around the manipulation of various individuals. Depending on the situation, different persuasion techniques are typically used.

Manipulation mastery I something that everyone wants to have. However, much goes into the final process before coming up with the final master plan. Men are manipulated in general by focusing more on what affects their masculinity. That is why, during most relationship breakups, partners tend to say hurtful words about their pair's masculinity. As a result, they end up making irrational decisions because they don't want to be belittled. This is a common manipulation technique that has resulted in unhealthy relationships that could have been avoided. Anyone who can manipulate you and make you feel inferior is extremely dangerous. Such people can impede your progress and make you feel as if your decision is unworthy. So, the best way to deal with such characters is to stand your ground by thinking clearly. Otherwise, you'll be their manipulation punching bag for the majority of the relationship.

Manipulation is also a long-term process. Most people want it to be as quick as possible. However, such a move yields only average results. The true art of manipulation necessitates patience and intrest. The person you are manipulating should be convinced that your way is the right way. Always keen on their emotions to know how they'll feel if the manipulation scheme goe wrong. A better way to accomplish this is to conduct exclusive research on their desires. This move enables you to devise a more workable manipulative plan. Take your time with this entire process, in other words. You won't like it when you're almost halfway through and your victim realizes the manipulation scheme. So be careful and do research before embarking on the entire manipulation process. It's a good idea to put yourself in your victims' shoes and get a unique idea of how they think. The best way is to research what they like and fear, then ue that against them during the manipulation scheme. It economizes

You are responsible for all of the problems that will arise if the victim realizes that your way of thinking does not conform to theirs. On the other hand, it enables you to plan well before embarking on the manipulation scheme.

Most manipulators frequently forget the concept of conforming to mother nature. It's a good idea to break the gravity rule and be flexible in your decision. In rainy climates, for example, it is wise to adjust by getting yourself an umbrella. In addition, on sunny days, we adjust by wearing light clothes for most functions. In short, do not be deluded into believing that your thought is the best regardless of your victim. This places you in a box of well-informed decisions. You won't believe it until you see that strange look on your victim's face. That's a clear indication that you're heading in the wrong direction, and you should adjust accordingly for the entire process to be a success. Different people have various personalities. So, when developing workable manipulation plans, it is critical to consider this crucial factor. Consult widely and understand the type of person you are attempting to manipulate. Understand how they respond to different types of environment. Check for their personal boundaries and keep out of that area.

So, how do you manipulate omeone without hurting their feelings? There are diferent maniplation techniques for each presented situation. In general, 90% of the people you'll try to manipulate prefer getting rewards at the end of their decion. What exactly does that imply? People do not want you to tell them what to do. Instead, enlighten the rewards of selecting a certain type of direction. ask them what they want and guide them to their 'own' decision path. Allow them to own the entire idea, only adjusting to what you believe is correct throughout the entire manipulation process. It is essential in all manipulation schemes to enable you, victims, to identify the indirect benefits of 'their' decision. For example, if you want your close one to lose weight, it would be inappropriate to talk about dieting as the main cause of excessive weight. Instead, inform them of the direct benefits of losing excess weight, such as having smoother skin and other advantages. This makes them feel as if they own the decision-making process and will frequently adjust to follow your ways. It also creates a good manipulation atmosphere for a fruitful course Make people thirsty before giving them water!

CHAPTER 2
Manipulation Techniques

Different manipulation techniques are used by predators on their victims. What's bizarre is that you can be manipulated without even knowing it. Most predators have mastered the art of manipulation and know when to strike unsuspecting victims. It is therefore wise that you be well conversant with some of these manipulation techniques. They save you the embarrassment of being manipulated without knowing it. These predators are closer than you can imagine. They have studied all of your moves and are aware of your weak points. Some of them are even family members, bosses, partners, or even friends. So, what are the diferent maniplation techniques that they ue to prey on their victims? Well, here's what you need to know about these maniplation tricks.

They Capitalize based on Your Will Power
Manipulators understand the importance of casting doubt on their victims. Most of the time, they'll let you know that every decision has ramifications. This trick allows you to weigh the available options, and you'll be surprised at how bad their consequences are. As a result, you'll have no choice but to tow down the manipulation line. To put it another way, the manipulators make you feel as if the decision was

yours. However, a keen analyzation of the direction picked will enable the victims to realize that they are doing more of the manipulator's wish than theirs. As a result, everyone must weigh their available options to ensure that they only choose what they truly desire. Always ensure that the benefits of that particular decion have a great IMPact on your wellbeing. Avoid making decisions to please other people. It places you in a box of manipulation, where you will be vulnerable in the hands of the predator.

The Round with Your Self-steem

Your self-esteem plays a huge. If you are belittled, you lose the morale of carrying out your duties.

Different tasks you can't even think straight if someone hurts your self-esteem. The majority of manipulators employ this technique to prey on unsuspecting victims. They know that if they mess with your self-esteem, you'll be more likely to give in to their pressure. As a result, they touch on the areas that degrade your self-esteem to a level that they can easily control your character.

It is thus prudent that you only associate with those who offer constructive criticism. Such people will help you carry a sucessful decision path that you'll carry all years. The simple lessons we learn from positive criticism are what help us become better people. Thus, anyone who corrects you intending to make you a better human is a keeper. Your enemies, on the other hand, capitalize on your low self-esteem to make you follow certain unworthy decisions. So, only hang out with those who offer constructive criticism.

The Major on DisqualificationS and Generalizations

Most predator make generalized statements that aren't backed up by any scientific event. There is an attempt to persuade their victims that they should follow 'workable ways' for fruitful results. The generalizations may cause the victims to rush in and make decisions that appear to favour the manipulators even more. However, if you come up with new ideas, they will dismiss them and urge you to change your way of thinking. This technique is very common among those who are emotionally attached to certain decisions. As a result, it ends up jeopardizing getting clear thoughts free of manipulation.

You must understand before making any decisions. If your ideology is disqualified, it does not mean that it is bad in general. Some people dismiss your ideas because they believe they are a threat to their success. As a result, they'll use negative comments to ensure that you change and follow them. If you pay attention to their ill-intention, you may lose sight of the overall goal and fail in the long run. But if you stick to your guns, you'll go a long way toward accomplishing what the manipulators thought was impossible.

You'll be surprised when they join you after determining that your path was correct.

Don't be afraid to bash out once in a while. Instead, take advantage of this opportunity to perfect your ideologies. The overall goal is to find workable solutions to the situation at hand. Always consult your inner self before making major decisions. Check it out and see if you're comfortable with the results of your decisions. Slowly outline the advantages of your way of thinking as opposed to the manipulators'. Don't put too much emphasis on pleasing anyone. Instead, be selfish enough to select what goes well with your ideologies.

You'll feel better when you realize your manipulators have no control over you. However, the journey to achieving this freedom is not a walk in the park. You should be willing to make some sacrifices and step outside of your comfort zone. Before deciding on a certain direction, consult widely. Those voices in your head could be correct. So, pay attention and get reasonable results from that inner voices. Don't let the manipulators convince you that you're not comfortable with your own decisions. They will seize such opportunities and make you feel bad about your constructive opinions. Instead, trust your conscience in everything you do. Sometimes, what you need to consult to make safer decions.

It is critical to maintaining calm in such situations. If manipulating predators try to persuade you to follow their ways, be sarcastic and tell the simple thank you. This will boost your confidence and make manipulators shy away from persuading you otherwise. That is the first hard step towards winning against cunning manipulators. Believe in your decisions and don't let anyone persuade you otherwise. Most of them simply want to take advantage of your vulnerability to get you to focus on less important priorities.

They hold Meaningless Conversations.
The first few minutes of a conversation should be enough to tell you that the other person doesn't care about your feelings. Most manipulators would like to focus all their attention on themselves.

Concerning the importance of simple conversation etiquette, they will make you feel as if your opinion doesn't matter if you try to express it. Remember that you are not in the pleasing-everybody buness. So, stay away from selfish individuals who don't understand conversation etiquette. It will benefit you more if they realize you aren't interested in their manipulative conversation.

On the other hand, the manipulators frequently give baseless conversations with the aim of wooing you into their sinister ideologies. There are no logical explanations behind their explanations. Most explanation raise more qestions than answers. As a result, they put their victims in a quandary about how to handle certain situations. That is when they push their agendas on unsuspecting victims. If you're wise enough, you'll recognize when the manipulators want to make a move to change your mind about certain principles. Don't be carried away by their meaningless conversations. Instead, make a very.

Make a habit of stopping the conversation when it does not benefit your character. It is recommended that you do not spend more than five minutes with a manipulator. This is because they will ensure that you accept their solution before leaving you in a bind. Nobody wants to be in a situation where they can't control the entire transaction, and you shouldn't be an exception. Champion your ideologies, and if the other party shows little concern, it's wise to cut the entire conversation for your sake. If you follow this step, you'll come out on top.

They infuse confusion and anguish in their victims
Most manipulative predators frequently say things that distort the way their victims think. Their decisions are unquestionable, and when you try to question their actions, they come up with ridiculous conclusions. They usually do this to make their victims feel inferior.

Following this, they will make their advances and impart crazy ideas to their victims. Also, they make their victims feel as if their opinions don't matter.

Dealing with such manipulators can be difficult for those with low self-esteem.

So, how can victims avoid such manipulative advantages? Well, it begins with understanding your role and the impact that individual decisions have on your life. Consider how it will affect the people around you, as well as, most importantly, yourself. In any situation, remember that your opinion matters more regardless of what others think. As long as your opinion does not affect anyone else, your way is the best way to go. Take a moment to consider what you will gain by standing your ground. Stop being a person who wants to please everyone all of the time. Even those whom you wish to please are wise enough to understand that they must come first before anything else.

We all make mistakes, but no one should make you feel like you owe them the entire world because of your mistakes in the past. When you allow everyone to judge everything you do, you become vulnerable to their thoughts and opinions. On the other hand, you'll feel less like a human being and may end up doing crazy things to appease your manipulators. But how does it benefit you if they have the last laugh while you're in a bad situation? So, always think about yourself before making any hasty decisions.

Have you ever wondered why you get so confused when someone brings back your past? You frequently feel so bad that you wish the ground would open and swallow you alive. But do they have power over your past? No! In most institutions, they were not even present in the first place. Manipulative predators want to make you feel like you hould have done something alter. However, they forget that your past is responsible for the person you are today. You couldn't have learned how to handle certain life situations wthout a past. You'd be more miserable if you didn't have a past.

So, stay away from people who believe you owe them an explanation about your past. Such people are simply frustrated and want to pass it on to unsuspecting victims. They'll do everything they can to ensure that their victims don't have much to say about their current situation. If you give such people a chance to tell you, they will.

If you don't know how to apply for your daily programs, you're in for a tough challenge. Pay no attention to their prejudgment tactics. Instead, concentrate on how you can become a better person who makes wise decisions in any situation or problem.

They misrepresent reality

Manipulative predators enjoy it when there is friction and misunderstanding among their victims. Most of them enjoy creating animosity in places where there is peace. They'll draft dubious schemes to create a hostile environment for their victims. The next step will be to peddle lies and make their victims fight over baseless schemes. They thrive on hostility and uncertainty, causing many victims to enter into unnecessary arguments with other unsuspected individuals. It is therefore very important to always do extensive research before getting into any argument. Check with the affected party for their side of the story. Don't believe anyone who tells you contradictory stories that will affect how you interact with others. Most of them do not believe that you should have a peaceful relationship. They'll thus bring in opposing ideas with the goal of destroying a once-beautiful relationship. The manipulative predator have no remorse! All they want to do is spread negativity to everyone so they don't have to suffer alone. When they see you having a successful relationship, they will devise evil ways to destroy such relationships. All they want is to share their bad moods with someone who isn't keen enough to notice their bad intentions.

Your point of view may differ from that of another person. Hence, don't let anyone drive conflicting thoughts that will affect your perception of a certain piece of information. Being peaceful keeps you out of a lot of trouble. It enables you to focus on essential duties that are necessary for a better relationship with everyone. On the other hand, it teaches you that not everyone reacts the same way to different situations. This, in turn, strengthens a peaceful transition with a steady relationship that benefits everyone.

If you make yourself vulnerable to manipulative actions, you will never have a successful relationship. A successful relationship is built on trust and listening to both sides of the story. However, most people make the mistake of falling prey to their manipulator's antics. In the end, they destroy relationships that may have taken many years to build. At that point, the manipulator will be overjoyed because you followed their instructions. Be smart in such situations and avoid making decisions based on flimsy claims. Make thorough research before making the final decision.

Manipulation is extremely hazardous to unsuspecting victims. It may drive them to depression, especially if their efforts are not appreciated. The manipulative predators don't have your best interest at heart. They will go out of their way to create confusion among unsuspecting victims. It is thus prudent to be wary of their manipulative methods to avoid becoming a victim of their actions. Always be careful and make a sober decion that hasdon't been influenced by the manipulator's tactics. Don't be the only one who is easily swayed into accepting unworthy thoughts. Also, be brave enough to let your manipulators know you're not buying into their antics.

CHAPTER 3
The Art of Persuasion

The art of persuasion ha changed over the years from simple techniques to more sophisticated ones. Unlike manipulation, persuasion is the act of persuading someone to do something that benefits both parties. It aids in achieving certain accomplishments that you can't achieve on your own. Almost everyone has been persuaded to take a particular detailed detailed detailed detailed detailed detailed detailed detailed det this is very familiar in the business world, where competitors come up with advertisement schemes to woo cutomers to the products that they are offering.

Persuasion techniques haven't changed many times in over 2,000 years. The approach may be different, but the persuasion tricks are simply an improvement on those used previously. Persuasion can also be defined as a catalyst that speeds up the process of getting work done on time. Its main goal is to achieve an outcome that you cannot achieve on your own. The overall result is something that benefits both parties and leaves them satisfied with the entire process. However, there are certain fundamentals that guide the persuasion principles. These fundamentals determine the success of any persuasion project. Persuasion is a practical art that needs polishing to ensure that the master is well-conversant with the tricks and tips that guide this process.

For a sucessful persuasion expedition, you must first understand the fundamentals of the process. The first step should be to research to ensure that you are on the same page with what needs to be done in this process. Before embarking on the persuasion path, always keenly analyze any situation. Why? This, in turn, prevents you from making common errors when attempting to persuade someone or a group of people.

You must also understand the goal of your persuasion journey. What do you hope to achieve? Realize the deliverables? Otherwise, what changes are you making to help this entire process? You should have a clear focus on your deliverables and ensure that you only pay attention to what can be achieved in a short period. Set realistic expectations to avoid disappointments throughout the process. Furthermore, be careful when making certain sensitive advances towards your persuasion journey. Any minor mistake can lead to misunderstanding between the parties involved, resulting in animosity that could have been avoided.

Why Is Persuasion an art?

This category is well-suited to art, which has a broad definition and persuasion. Many people forget that persuading someone necessitates expertise. It necessitates that all parties involved be sober when making certain decisions. It is always critical to analyze the impact of persuasive advances on potential parties. So, what attributes make persuasion an art? Or, what are the fundamentals that surround the art of persuasion, and what can be done to improve it? Here are some philosophical attributes that affirm that persuasion I an art that necessitates expertise.

It elicits strong emotions

It is difficult to persuade someone. However, when the process is sucessful, the parties involved have an outburst of emotions. That is why it is extremely crucial that you only state facts when persuading an individual to go a particular way. Always look forward to the benefits of working together on a fruitful course. This enables parties to form an amicable environment that benefits a fruitful relationship for a sucessful persuasion scheme. On the other hand, it establishes a strong relationship between the parties involved. As a result, the fact that persuasion elicits emotions makes it an excellent art for persuading individuals to follow a certain direction.

It expresses an Individual's Point of View

Art has the ability to convey an individual's point of view without any conveyance. Persuasion opens different angles of thought, and the parties need to be extremely careful when convincing each other. It needs respect on both sides the person attempting to persuade another person should concentrate on the emotional consequences of their persuasion scheme. They must ensure that they do not compromise on the overall objective while attempting to push through their agendas. It creates a peaceful envy for amicable understanding.

It comes with an authentic message

Every art should be distinct and one-of-a-kind. The same holds for persuasion. Persuasion techniques must be distinct to woo potential victims in a specific direction. It also conveys an authentic message that is distinct enough to help the involved parties identify troubling issues within the school. To be persuasive, you must identify certain points that your victim lacks and capitalize on them for a fruitful course of action. Persuasion always creates an artistic impression of the situation at hand. As a result, it shouldn't just be a person's exaggeration of what needs to be done.

Persuasion is an important skill that everyone should have. Almost every individual has been n a place and tme where they had to persuade someone for something. This is especially common in sucessful companies that need to persuade their employees that they need to work extra hard to achieve certain goals. The beauty of this art is that anyone interested can learn the necessary skills. As an employee, you should have persuasion techniques to persuade your boss to pay you better wages. Every day, new situations arise in which we must persuade others to give us a listening ear.

The same applies to salespeople who need to people to buy their products. In such a scenario, you must be exceptionally smart to entice potential clients to your business products. The business world has stiff competition, and thus anyone who does not have excellent persuasion skills will definitely get there. That is why it is always critical to developing breathtaking persuasion skills that your competitors do not have. This enables to keep up with the cutthroat competition that every market has.

Practising the Art of Persuasion
Though persuasion is difficult, anyone who develops interest can do so comfortably. We all want to be in a position where we can persuade people to do things that will benefit both parties. But how much are you willing to sacrifice for the persuasion venture to succeed? It is not an easy task, as many people believe. It necessitates patience and commitment while focusing on the big picture. Set your eyes on the persuasion venture and be ready to adjust so that the venture becomes successful. Don't be rigid in your thinking. Instead, be flexible and make any necessary adjustments that favor your persuasion journey.

The art of persuasion is not hereditary, as some belief. However, your environment determines whether the enterpress will be a success or a failure. Positive energy all through persuasion needs to be energy all through persuasion needs to be energy all through persuasion needs to Avoid negative criticisms that cause you to lose focus on the overall price. Surround yourself with people who inspire you to better in your persuasion venture. Ask them what they think should change and work toward achieving your overall goal. This keeps you focused on the entire persuasion journey.

Here's what you should do if you're practising the art of persuasion:

Asses the Persuasion Environment
One mistake you should avoid is underestimating your audience. Every audience has its distinct approach. As a result, assuming that your persuasion tactics will produce the same results across different audiences is incorrect. It is therefore critical that you conduct research and understand what your target audience requires. serves their age and social background This gives you a given idea of the workable techniques that you should apply with the audience. On the other hand, it gives you the confidence to approach the audience because you already know their weak spot.

Convincing someone necessitates far more research than most people believe. It begins by putting yourself in the shoes of your audience to better understand them. What excites them? What does your audience dread? How much are they willing to part with to be comfortable? Are there any social or religious ties that prevent them from engaging in certain practices? These questions should give you a general idea of the type of audience you want to persuade. It enlightens your audience's weak spot. After that, you can capitalize on the available information to make your advances.

Aside from that, knowing your audience gives you a better idea of what you should talk about. It's always a good idea to stay within your audience's comfort zone. They may find this provocative and, as a result, frustrate your persuasive advances. Don't be a person who makes a lot of assumptions when it comes to pleasing the audience. Be wary of those who get excited in the first few minutes of a persuasion venture without getting clear details of your presentation. They might be putting you in a trap that will be difficult to get out of because of your ignorance. In short, conduct extensive research before approaching any audience.

Examine Your Subjects' Self-steem

Why are people with low self-esteem so easy to persuade? Well, this general of people have less confidence in expressing their their their their their their their their their their their their They'd rather wait for other people to come up with ideas before acting on them. This makes them vulnerable to persuasion because most of them will accept almost anything without thoroughly researching the consequences. As a result, you should always confirm if such people exist in your target audience. If you find them vulnerable, seize the opportunity and pass your agenda.

Be careful, though, and don't assume that quiet people have low self-esteem. Such people typically do more listening but talk less. However, before accepting your ideologies, they usually conduct extensive research on their own. As a result, it is incorrect to classify everyone who is inactive as having low self-esteem. Surprisingly, these

People may surprise you with facts you hadn't considered before. In your research, go through each point and assess its strengths and weaknesses. Put yourself in a position to answer any questions that may arise during the persuasion venture.

Why is it difficult to persuade your group members?

When you have to persuade a group of people to go against their principles, persuasion becomes a little more difficult. Why is this the case? Well, when you were in the group, you believed in how everything was done. Changing your mind about the group's leadership structure and principles, hence, may put you in a difficult battle. Some members will side with you, while a huge section will try to jeopardize your persuasion advances. In such cases, it is preferable to provide the audience with facts as to why they should follow your ideologies.

It's a good idea to schedule meetings with each of the group members to figure out why some of them aren't buying into your ideas.

This will give you a good idea of what you're doing wrong and allow you to make any necessary adjustments before the big day. Always seek advice from those who have travelled the same path as you. ask them how they managed the diferent challenges that they presented themselves along the way. Such benchmarks will educate you on the basis of persuasion as well as what should be avoided for a fruitful course. Everyone wants a smooth sail, but with persuasion, you'll have to go the extra mile to find it.

Dealing with group members necessitates patience and dedication. Don't be in a hurry to get fast results. Always remember the breauty of hard work and persistence in your persuasion adventure. Consult with a variety of people to gain a better understanding of how to deal with specific members of the group. Also, listen to everyone's opinions and determine your strengths and weaknesses. Persuasion warrior enters the battlefield prepared for what may happen ahead. Such a move necessitates intensive preparation before the final persuasion battle.

Why Should You Be Agressive
Because there is a lot of competition in this field, persuasion necessitates agreement. If you are not willing to take a risk and go head-to-head with the audience, another person will come in and take your place. The art of persuasion favors those who are willing to be aggressive in their research as they seek to know their audience better. You should have the detail of the potential audience at your fingertips. However, this does not happen as easily as many people expect. You'll need to be prepared and outperform all of your competitors.

Many victims fell for the bait of smooth talkers who know how to persuade their audience. The art of persuasion necessitates that you relate to your audience in a variety of ways. You must know what to say in a variety of situations when confronted with a difficult task. That is why being aggressive is very crucial, especially when speaking to someone for the first time. First impressions are also important in persuasion. The audience will hold you in high regard if you can woo them with your persuasion antics on the first encounter. As a result, you should be well-prepared to face the audience with confidence.

Different audiences necessitate diferent approach mechanisms. What stands out is that aggressive suitors find it easier to juggle between different audiences. Being aggressive gives one a sense of belonging when dealing with different audiences. The majority of audiences want to identify with their suitors. So, be smart and research what can make you acceptable in the eyes of your target audience. It is the small adjustments that make one sucessful in their persuasion venture. When making persuasion advances, never underestimate the will of people. Instead, be an avid listener and only speak when you've planned everything on how you'll handle the audience.

The beauty of persuasion is that it can be tailored to meet the needs of a specific audience. Remember that your audience should be your top priority. As a result, anything that harms the audience should be avoided at all costs. On the other hand, people will easily notice when you deviate from the main course Always stick to your plans and make changes only if they will provide accurate results for what you want to achieve. Just a reminder that you should be in charge of the entire persuasion journey. This enables you to identify what isn't working for excellent results.

Why is a good introduction important?
The first few minutes of a conversation determine whether or not you will win the target audience. Most of the time, suitors forget that the art of persuasion relies heavily on the ability to persuade a stranger within the first few minutes of the conversation. As a result, putting on a bad show may result in your space being taken over by the competition. A quick tip is to make a list of what you want to tell the audience. This will give you an orderly way of going through your persuasion maneuvers.

Persuasion is an art that necessitates unique presentations. What makes you stand out from your competitors? Is your delivery impressing the audience? If not, what are you doing to ensure you get the best results? Having a clear focus on the overall goal plays a huge role in determining how you'll impressively convince the audience. We all want a piece of the cake, but are we ready to make exemplary first impressions? The best way to be unique is to practice your approach antics before your presentation D-day. You'll gain a better understanding of the type of audience you'll be dealing with when the occasion arrives.

Another quick reminder: don't appear disorganized during your first encounter with the audience. Nobody likes someone who doesn't know what they're talking about. Being disorganized distastes the target audience and makes them vulnerable to grabs by your competitors. Always remember that some have been waiting for you for a long time, and if you mess up, they will be more than willing to take your market share. So, deliver a smooth presentation during the first few minutes of encountering the audience. It's well worth it!

Capitalize on ocial Inadequacy

According to research, it is easier to persuade those who are socially inadequate. In a normal conversation, such individuals frequently don't have much to say. They'd rather follow the advice of their'mentors' on certain issues. So, keenly study the target audience and establish their characteristics. Check to see if the audience easily accepts the opinions of those they regard as superior.' If so, seize this opportunity and forward your agenda while they are still vulnerable. Social inadequacy is an excellent opportunity for suitors who are embarking on their first persuasion venture.

As a result, you should conduct extensive research on the behaviours of your target audience. Confirm what necessitates a capitalize on such. Also, don't make hurried decisions when dealing with such audiences. Instead, be patient enough to know which areas to avoid during the presentation. During your presentation, it is critical that you only focus on the audience's requements. It allows you to pay more attention to the dos and don'ts of any specific audience. You'll realize that a few minutes into the persuasion adventure, you'll be bombarded with familiar questions. You should carefully give responses that befit your advances in such circumstances.

Socially inadequate people frequently rely upon on'mentors' when making decisions. It is therefore critical that you identify the mentors in an audience. Push your agendas throughout the audience to persuade them to follow your antics. Most buness brands ue this inadvertently without realizing it. By incorporating social influencers into your marketing strategy, you'll be a close distance from makeng a sucessful imact. Some people will buy products because they can relate to their favourite celebrities. As a result, you should employ this tactic to garner a sizable following during your persuasion venture. It makes persuading people much easier.

Why Should You Be a Powerful Listener

You should never underestimate the power of being an average listener. Most politicians have mastered the art of persuasion by simply telling people what they want to hear. Listening to your audience allows you to gather enough information to use during your persuasion venture. But how does one become an avid listener? Simply pay attention to your audience and figure out what they want. Following that, you can plan well on how to achieve their objectives. Listening is a powerful tool in the art of persuasion that should not be underestimated.

Candidates in the political world-first research potential voters. Before launching a campaign, they send a research team to establish what voters want. Following that, the coin a manifesto aligns with the priorities of the voters. As a result, potential voters believe that politician understands their problems and is one of them. Successful politicians have mastered the art of listening and can thus persuade a large number of people to vote for them during elections. To be sucessful in your persuasion venture, you should prioritize listening to your audience's requirements before making any advances in your persuasion pursuit.

You'll amass a sizable following if you have strong listening skills. Nobody wants to follow the antics of people they can't relate to during difficult times. As a result, always consider what your audience wants. Gather a few people to state their requirements. Following that, work tirelessly to ensure that their needs are met within the required time frame. Moreover, before making any persuasion advances, consult widely. This enables you to familiarize yourself with the audience, making it easier to understand what they require. Don't be the only one who makes assumptions. Instead, give your audience a listening ear to better serve them.

Mastering the Art of Persuasion

Introducing a product or idea to an audience I not enough. You must go a long way to ensure that they accept your ideologies. Otherwise, your persuasion venture will not result in a fruitful outcome. You need to spice things up for credibility introduction through the use of persuasion techniques This is especially crial for entrepreneurs who have buness ideas that they want to accomplish. Your target market may be full of other competitors who are approaching prospective customers in a different manner. You should always conduct research and note what you are not doing correctly. In most cases, the persuasion techniques you're employing need to be changed. After that, you'll have a smooth sail in your persuasion adventure.

Here are the seven steps you should take to master the art of manipulation:

1. Remind Your Audience of The Benefits of Your Products Consistently

Most entrepreneurs believe that advertisements have to be done once. However, sucessful business brands such as Coca-Cola and Pepsi have demonstrated that repetition is key in persuading customers. You should imitate these tactics and constantly remind your potential customers about the product you're offering. It helps them identify with your product more clearly. Also, notify them of any packaging changes so that they are not perplexed when looking for their favorite product at the store.

Advertisement is a persuasion ingredient. In fact, not a lot of people are aware that they are being persuaded to buy certain products when they watch or read the advertisements. All they care about is how interesting or captivating the advertisement is in comparison to that of available competitors. People frequently like to identify with products that give them the value of their money. As a result, it is extremely important that you always focus on delivering the best to your potential customers. It encourages them to remain loyal to the brand and even invite other customers. A successful business relies on referrals from existing customers.

2.   Be Flexible During Your Presentation

You should not have a rigid way of thinking when introducing a product to a certain group of people. Different customers have diferent requirements. It is thus absurd to assume that they will react in the same manner. That is why it is very essential to do thorough research on the type of audience that you are targeting. Know their limits and work hard not to exceed them. Consider their culture and religious beliefs when making persuasion advances. It gives them a sense of belonging to your persuasion campaign. You don't want any conflicts with your target audience, so be aware of what they consider viable and adhere to providing exceptional services.

Also, the information you are spreading to your audience should be in the context of your products. Do not mislead your audience by making false declarations. Your target cutomer are very sensitive, and anything that jeopardizes quality delivery is a no! Don't be in a hurry to make quick sales while not providing ideal items. When they realize this sinister move, your products will face backlash, and it can get worse when you have to deal with legal authorities because of your mischief.

3. Use Diverse Storylines to Drive Your Point Home

People are more likely to buy into your ideas when they are convinced by an authentic story, according to research. In fact, potential cutomers believe more in contrasting story scenarios than statements of facts about a particular product. As a result, it is advisable that during your presentation, you give relevant examples about the workability of the product you're offering. This gives the audience a brief idea that they'll experience similar results if they try that product. On the other hand, it instills confidence in trying out the product because they want to be part of the class of sucessful people who are trying out that particular product.

However, it is critical that you only provide accurate information in your storylines. Don't write fictitious stories that don't have any authentic background. Some customers may go the extra mile and conduct research to confirm the veracity of your story. Furthermore, your competitors may wish to interfere by poking you draws attention to the authenticity of your fictitious story. If they discover that it does not add up, they will be more than willing to share it with the audience so that your products are dismissed for providing false testimonials.

4. Personalize Your Presentation to Feature Receiver's Background

Your approach should differ depending on the type of audience and their background. For example, if your audience is intuitive and creative, you cannot use the same approach. That is why, before making any persuasion advances, you must first study the audience. Take your time and figure out what kind of services they require the most. After that, prepare a presentation that will cut through the audience by providing relevant information that benefits their stature. The next step is to ensure that you answer all of their questions correctly.

Always create a personal relationship with the audience before making your persuasion advances. It enables you to comprehend their way of thinking. It also allows the audience to feel included in your persuasion strategy. Your target audience should be able to relate to the type of product you're offering. A personal relationship ensures that both parties are thinking on the same level. As a result, you'll find it simple to persuade them to take a particular path. On the plus side, it allows you to adequately prepare for some of the questions that may arise during the presentation.

5. Use Their Mentors to Introduce Them

People are more likely to be persuaded if a new person is introduced to them by someone they know. The majority of audiences want a sense of belonging in any product presentation. As a result, when a mentor introduces you to his/her people, you'll find it easy to persuade them to adopt your ideologies. As a result, before approaching an audience, conduct some research and identify the person to whom they relate the most. After that, speak with that individual and reach an agreement on the terms and terms for them to introduce you to the prospective audience. Ensure that you seize that opportunity by providing exceptional service delivery.

We all want a smooth and easy persuasion presentation. Sometime, you'll have to identify with the person that the audience relates the most. They make the persuasion scheme easier because the audience will listen to you more. However, a mere introduction does not imply that the audience will buy your ideologies if they are not presented in a amicable way. Following the introduction, the ball is simply in your court. Everything you do from now on will determine whether or not the audience will be wooed to your ideologies or products.

## 6.	Materialize Your Idea Using a Prototype or Demo

What you see is not the same as what your audience sees. As a result, it is incorrect to assume that simply making expressions during the presentation will persuade your audience. The best way to deal with this problem is to create a demo or prototype. People are more likely to buy into an idea that they can touch and feel. The demo makes it easier for the prospective audience to be on the same level as the presentation. It also makes the explanation of detailed information a little better.

Most presentations are sucessful due to less sophisticated demos or prototypes. Your prototype should not be complicated. It should be written in such a way that the audience can easily understand the concept you're attempting to advance. Don't put too much emphasis on making the prototype unique if it won't meet the overall goal of simplicity. Thus, go through the available options and select the one that produces a less complex prototype. Then, design the prototype to meet the needs of the current world. After that, you should have an easier time convincing potential customers to buy into your ideas.

## 7.	Use Social Media to Demonstrate Interest

Over the years, social media has transitioned to be a very potent marketing tool. What's more exciting is that you don't have to spend a lot of money to reach a large audience. As a result, you should concentrate on this wonderful marketing tool to persuade your audience. Target 1000 social media users to give out excellent testimonials about your products and services. This alone is sufficient to persuade the target audience that you have exceptional products and services. People prefer to buy what they can relate to and for which they have proof of interest.

Most investors want to fund projects that excite people. Having a sized social media following of people who like your ideas may be excellent in persuading them to invest in your ideologies. However, creating such a massive following necessitates patience and dedication. Your followers need to find something interesting and relatable to them. As a result, you should be cautious and only provide them with authentic products and services. It won't be long before they refer your exemplary services to their friends and close family members.

The art of persuasion I something that anyone can have as long as they have a deep interest. When persuading an audience, it is critical to understand their needs and focus on satisfying them. It is also critical to avoid underestimating any audience while making persuasion advances. This saves you the embarrassment of being bashed by the audience when they realize your persuasion techniques aren't working on them. Also, ensure that your products are authentic and do not exceed the limits of your audience. Respecting the limits of your target audience ensures a smooth personal relationship that leads to positive results. As a result, follow the abovemented guidelines for an effective persuasion adventure.

CHAPTER 4
How to Use Different Manipulative Techniques to Own Your Emotions and Personal Relationships

What exactly is maniplation? When someone says manipulation, a lot of ideas or what it means come to mind. According to the Cambridge Dictionary, manipulation is the act of controlling or influencing someone or something to your merit, which is always unfair. Many people all over the world believe that manipulative behaviour is wrong. It is also known that something that has disadvantages also has advantages; it all depends on how you play your cards. People use a variety of manipulative techniques to get you to do what they want. Toxic people can use them to gain an advantage in relationships. The following are clinical analyses of various manipulative techniques designed to trap people in relationships and emotions.

Feelings of Guilt and Sympathy

Guilt and Sympathy can also be categorized as motival Blackmail. It's the most common technique used in personal relationships, and it goes unnoticed a lot of the time. People are compelled to do things or do favours for a partner as he bargains with your feelings for him. This is since it always works. This type of manipulation can continue indefinitely until the victim decides she's had enough. Partners have unhealthy relationships as a result of emotional blackmail. During arguments, the partner ues threats or fear to have her way. Statements like "if you leave me, I would rather commit suicide than let you be with someone else" are common in a relationship. Such words make you feel guilty about what will happen if you choose your path.

Sometimes sympathy and guilt are used to exploit the emotions of people who are not in a relationship. The act of doing well always trumps our emotions. As humans, we always feel bad for people who are in difficult situations. We've come together to help someone who has required many people feel carryed after carrying out humanitarian work.

In such cases, you should ask yourself some serious questions and think deeply about your life. Being in a relationship because someone threatened to kill himself is not a viable option. Do not fall for it when such statements are uttered. It's frequently a manipulation tactic and a cold threat by the individual. You should understand where to draw the line. Be a selfish once and think about yourself.

Criticism

This is why the manipulator employs tactics like belittling, dismissing, and ridiculing you. This throws someone off-balance. Negative criticism is directed at a participant, making them feel unworthy. The act of criticizing allows them to gain control of you. The manipulator creates a narrative in which there is always something wrong with you and you are not good enough. This type of narrative makes you doubt yourself frequently about what you feel and know. It reaches a point where you no longer trust yourself.

Manipulators exploit your vulnerabilities against you. Most of the time, they consciously create relationships with insecure partners. They make you believe they are always right and you are always wrong. Constant criticism from the manipulator gives them superiority over you. Their criticism is always negative, and they make it sound as if they have your best interests at heart. Giving positive feedback where due I hard to come by.

When you don't feel like you're in a relationship, that's a red flag. In a healthy relationship, someone should be free to express themselves and should not have feelings of marginalization. If you realize this, take the appropriate action of walking out of that relationship. Never look back on it.

Using Flattery, Kindness, and Charm

The use of kindness, charm, and flattery is frequently more damagery than realized. The generous deployment of these techniques known as a passive-aggressive behavior type The manipulator employs tactics such as gifting someone items, massaging their egos with flattery, and a slew of compliments. One is left to realize the real reason behind the compliments, expensive gifts, and paying attention to the victim. These are actions taken with ulterior motives, especially when they realize you're about to catch up on the manipulative state.

Bribery is another technique of manipulating someone. When implemented, it yields result. Bribery I a better technique than blackmailing an individual. You can entice a friend with a better offer. The reward does weren't have to be monetary valuable. It can be something you would have done anyway or had already done previously. Perhaps, in the process of asking a colleague for help in your studies, you can decide to offer her a lunch treat after studying in exchange.

Determine what the individual truly requires. Once you've determined the person's need, you should try and give it to the person. If one of your friends has a crush on one of your schoolmates, you should promise your friend that you will obtain the schoolmate's phone number.

When ung flattery or kindness, make ure you don't make it obvious. Just make it appear a if you are determined to do something nice for the friend.

When you notice manipulation, do not accept their gifts or succumb to their compliments. These are not genuine acts of kindness, but rather methods used to lure you back in. Remember, they're only doing these things to "get" the conditional love that isn't there.

Gaslighting

Gaslighting is a manipulation technique that causes the victim to question his mental state. It's a very insidious technique used by manipulators. The most common question that arises from Gaslighting is, "Are you normal?" The partner alway refutes claims of using such words or even doing what you accuse him of, omitting information and twisting words in his favour Manipulators will also try to push the narrative of losing your mind. The manipulator can talk to you in a way that implies he knows what is best for you. The constant questioning of their knowledge and the act of undermining instincts.

When this act is repeated, it eats the ability of one to trust her brain to know if he is being mistreated by her partner. The victim is convinced that she requires the manipulator's assistance to stay on track. The victim, on the other hand, can overcome this technique if she keeps a journal of activities unfolding and even sharing with friends.

Lying

Lying is a common tactic used by con artists. Manipulators lie in almost everything they see, hear, or know. They concoct a slew of lies that are so complex that they tend to wrap people into believing they can't tell the difference between reality and fake life. These lies can only be refuted by looking for inconsistencies in the stories. When a deal is too good to pass up, think twice before accepting an offer. Bus drivers use this manipulation technique because they have no concerns about it. Lying can be caught if the victim decides to a background check on the sources of information.

The Advantage of Having a Home Court

The process of manipulating an individual is entirely dependent on the level of control one has over the other. manipulator will insist on meeting and having your interactions in an area he is familiar with. This technique I ued to gain an edge of control over someone by taking them out of their element. The places where you normally spend your time are usually his and not yours. These locations include his office, home, vehicle, and hanging out joints. Such areas allow the manipulator to assert his dominance. When someone is uneasy with the environment, he is easy to control.

This technique can be done away with the victim makes it clear that meeting places are where they are both comfortable. Both of you choose restaurants and events to attend. This results in a joint partnership between the two of you. In the process of breeding a healthy relationship.

Caressing the move

Caring for one's ego is most common in interpersonal relationships. The manipulator caresses the victim ego by feeding her lies every time. The ego develops over time, and in the end, the manipulator has you on his leash. This technique can be avoided if the victim of the act possessessessessessessessessessessessessessessessessessessessess

Making Unusual Requests Before Your Real Request

This type of manipulation technique is based on a "mind game." The tactic entails asking an unusual request, motly of a higher degree. This throws the person off balance because he wasn't expecting such a request. The manipulator knew how that person was likely to respond, he would have asked for the usual request such as money, favor, shoes. The victim was more likely to say no. This is because people's minds have been trained to avoid these tasks.

For example, a salesperson knows that approaching someone on the street and asking him to buy the items being sold will most likely lead to no sale. The salesman would first ask the potential client to do something for him, such as help him directions. This creates a "relationship" with the person and makes it less likely that they will reject your presentation.

Irate Outbursts and Voice Raising

During arguments, manipulators raise their voices to intimidate someone. They believed that raising the voice agressively or loudly can enable them to achieve what they wanted. In a relationship, passion can manifest itself in various ways, such as tenderness, cute smiles you give one another, laughter, and the desire to share warmth in the arms of another. Passion, however, however, howev should not be mistaken by anry unpredictable outbursts dure debate. In marriages or couples, one person tends to disagree with the other. It is not unusual. There are numerous ways to handle conflict; having healthy communication with your partner is one such scenario, rather than screaming or temper tantrums. Strong body language sometimes accompanies the aggressive voice.

The manipulator can also begin to select quarrels of non-issues. When this happens, it's a warning sign that something needs to be worked out. There are forces at work. Someone who picks random quarrels in a relationship is either cheating on the partner or looking to end the relationship.

When the couple is around friends and family, manipulators tend to appear calm, cool, and collected. The moment family members have gone the angry outbursts and raise of the voice are witnessed. Even if a partner is in the wrong, one must disagree without displaying violent tendencies. Provide constructive criticism or speak politely to the partner. The line should be drawn between being passionate and being abusive. While there are certain types of manipulators who, when a negative event happens, a conflict arises, or things seem to be in chaos, the person becomes super calm. This can also be a manipulation technique. It creates an impression of overreacting by the victim, especially by making you feel as if you can't trust your emotional reactions.

Manipulators can thus control their partner's emotional responses. The victim expected a response from the manipulator that she was unable to obtain. He determines whether a situation necessitates an emotional response from the intended victim or if it is simply considered dramatic. The manipulator demonstrates more calmness, coolness, and collected than was expected.

Fear over a Partner then Relief

This manipulation technique has a high rate of sucess over its victims. It usually entails making someone fearful that the worst will happen. Making up stories or spreading misinformation

If the story doesn't happen, that person is likely to be relieved, and he would be happy enough to grant you whatever you want. It's all about playing mental games on the victim.

Play the Victim Role

This type of manipulation of playing the victim is a great way of achieving what you wanted. As long as the manipulator does not overdo it. This tactic should only be used once in a while. If the act is done regularly, it is likely to result in excellent results. There are numerous ways of playing a victim card; it all depends on acting as a wonderful person. The manipulator has the option of exaggerating or imagining personal issues, inflating or imagining health issues, and also co-dependence. This technique entails a person acting deliberately as bereaved to elicit sympathy and favour from his/her victims. He/she can play weak or even powerless. The manipulator will then play the role of the victim to gain empathy and concern from his/her victims and the people around him/her. Humans are naturally drawn to carry out charity work for people who are suffering. Most manipulators employ these techniques in a relationship. When the manipulator gets into a fight with the partner, negative energy was omitted, things ware said, and the partner is just heartbroken. She is overwhelmed by how you've hurt her in such away.

In many cases, the victim is the one who always apologizes. Even if she wasn't at fault or didn't cause the problem. When helpless, the partner always needs extra love and attention. It's made to make you feel less worthless in the relationship and a bad partner. This allows the partner to avoid accepting responsibility for their actions. The main reason for using victimhood tactics is to exploit the victims' goodwill, guilt-tripping, and explore their sense of duty and obligation. It is also to extract protective and nurturing instincts from the recipients, which leads to getting unreasonable benefits and concessions.

Make use of logic and statistics.

To persuade the partner, this manipulation technique employs statistics and logic. When dealing with rational-minded people, logic is the most effective persuasion tool. The manipulator brings at least four results-oriented explanations as to why the thing he wants would benefit he and the person being asked. The presentation should be carried out in a rational and calm manner while you present your case. Ensure that you do not lose your temper at any point, even if difficult questions are raised or a disagreement arises. To be able to seal the deal and get a rational person on your side, you must keep your emotions in check during the presentation, or you will not be able to achieve what you want.

There are several manipulators who encourage "intellectual bullying." They believe that they have expertise and in-depth in certain areas. With this in mind, they will take advantage of you by proposing alleged facts, statistics, and any other data you may have very little know about. This tends to happen in organizations and departments, social and relational arguments, sales departments and areas of financial needs, professional

The manipulators' act of being an expert in that field will give them power over you. The individual hopes to persuade you with their agenda in a convincing manner. Most manipulators rely on this technique just to exercise and feel a sense of intellectual superiority. This manipulative technique can be overcome by acting as if what you require is the only logical thing to do.

Campaigns for Smear Campaigns

This manipulative technique is ued in scenarios where the manipulator is unable to control the way you view yourself. As a result, they want to start controlling how other people see you; they will always play the victim because you are being labelled the toxic person. This tendency is typically associated with politians. They twist the facts to suit themselves and their egos. This act of spinning the truth is mostly used by predators to camouflage bad behaviour.

Your partner's campaign is an arrogation strike to destroy her/her victim's reputation.

Dumb and not Breaking Character

When the act has been detected, a technique employed is a not breaking character. Do not break character if your method is being discovered and your partner, co-worker, or friend calls you out on using a manipulative technique on them. When these people call you out for being a liar, they tend to be extremely upset than you actually are, and they don't even acknowledge that it's true. Alternatively, you can employ the classic "playing dumb" tactic. For manipulators, the easiest way he is likely to manipulate a person is by denying the they are accused of. If the friend persists, you should appear even more hurt. The individual needs to blame the problem on the friend, which will make the individual feel even more sorry and guilty for you.

Other methods of manipulative technique are feigning ignorance. The manipulator passive- aggressively makes you take on what is her delivery. This technique is mostly used by some children as a tactic to manipulate and delay their parents into doing something they do not want to do. Couples will also use this tactic on their partners when they have responsibilities that they do not want to carry out or when they have something to hide.

Projection

Manipulators tend to believe that all of the bad things that happen to them and the unpleasantness that surrounds them are the faults of someone else. This is referred to as projection. Normal people do it a little, but the manipulators do it a lot. Projection is a defense mechanism deployed to displace a sense of responsibility for the manipulator's bad behavior and traits by projecting them to other people. The solution to this technique is to refrain from developing your own sense of empathy or compassion onto a manipulator and not owning any of the individual person's projects either.

Being Sarcastic and Making Negative Jokes

Most manipulators prefer to make critical statements, which are frequently passed out as humour or sarcasm. Their main goal is to make you feel belittled, insecure, and unworthy. There are many ways they do this, such as making a variety of comments ranging from the partner's appearance, the type of phone you use, to your family background and credentials. The manipulator does this in the hopes of imposing emotional superiority over the partner by making you look bad around your colleagues or friends, and getting you to actually lose your morale. In front of others, the manipulator tends to be sarcastic about their victim. When they carry out this act, the victim's self-esteem suffers a major blow. They also do this to demonstrate to other people how trustworthy they are.

When the manipulator says hurtful things to the victim, it's not their fault because it was all a joke. Even if the jokes are cruel, it doesn't matter. It only reveals that the victim is overly sensitive and incapable of handling dark humour. The jokes can also be made about you in public places and front of your family. case where a victim responds in a negative manner in front of other people, the manipulator will then make you think you are ruining the fun or making a scene. This tactic is used to avoid taking responsibility for the unfolding scenarios.

This manipulative technique can be ued in a personal relationship. The victim can handle the situation by not being overly sensitive or ruining the fun. Confronting a partner can be a hard task, especially if they have caused you pain, and in the process, you risk appearing like a bad person. Being able to stand up for oneself, on the other hand, is essential. Even if the manipulator will almost certainly try to shame you for it. The sooner you can recognize manipulative behaviours, the sooner you will be able to put an end to them.

Constantly calling and texting to check-in

When your calls and texts go unanswered, it's natural to feel disgusted. The act of ghosting someone causes a great deal of annoyance. When communication between you and your partner starts to feel obvious and it entails the partner constantly asking to know your whereabouts, what you are doing at the moment, and to know who you are with at all.

If your better half tends to get upset whenever you don't pick their calls, they may want you to believe it's mainly becaue they have missed you. However, this is a lie because missing someone does not entail making a partner feel guilty in order to have their phone all the time.

Manipulators ue the technique of silent treatment alo. They never respond to a partner's calls and text messages. They gain authority by making the victim wait in the proceses.

Insulting and requesting Forgiveneness after the Act

People sometimes believe that for a partner to be insulted, only one derogatory word must be used for their language to be considered unacceptable. The act of calling your significant other "pathetic" or "stupid" is an insult. Abuse is believed to be name-calling and using swear words against partners. Following the manipulators' outburst, they return to plead for forgiveness. They put on a show of trying to get back on your good side with lovely gestures.

Individuals will claim that they used disrespectful words because they were caught up at the moment and were simply expressing fervid intense emotions.

The relationship will feel extremely dramatic if the outburst lead to an abusive cycle. The manipulator can hide their behavior for some time after successfully winning you back, but the outburst is likely to occur again.

Making the partner believe that what you want is also what she wants

Most relationships begin with making commitments to each other. With requirements and deal breakers as part of the process. Compromises are made as the relationship progresses and you begin to merge your lives together. That is a normal occurrence in a healthy relationship. However, it is not recommended for a partner to set aside everything that they want and need to appease the other significant one. The needs of a manipulator are being met far more frequently than the needs of the victims in the relationship.

Refusing to Leave a Partner's Personal Space

Couples should have some personal spaces in a healthy relationship. manipulator will leave your bedside, apartment, or any type of personal space until they have attained what they want or need Some couples believe that the act of always wanting to be with you is a form of romance. It is not the case. When someone is standing at your door and you ask them to leave you alone and they do not move an inch. You later agree to let them into your home. However, you should never misinterpret their action as romance or devotion. Respecting each other's boundaries results in a healthy relationship. Manipulators will always try to control the people with whom you will spend time.

Partners are not superved to be our everything, especially in monogamous relationships. Couples require friends and personal social networks. Managing each other's social lives out of romantic relationships will help make these relationships stronger and stronger.

Partners should avoid getting in the way of their significant other friendships by attacking or criticizing the people they choose to hang out with.

Manipulators frequently ask victims to forego social plans, spy on victims by checking in incessantly when they are with other people.

Imposing one's insecurities on the victim

Manipulators routinely impose their insecurities on the victim of manipulation. This is typically done to control how they react to manipulators. Several excuses are used to justify the reasons for the act. The manipulator will ue a number of reasons like they have cheated on before, and that is the main reason why they do not want their significant other to have "I'm sorry, I didn't mean to act that way, but I'm so worried about you leaving me!" is simply a pretext that manipulators ue frequently, especially when they want to point out flaws in their actions. They do this to focus all of your attention on their actions and thus gain complete control over you.

In a healthy relationship, there is an acceptable line between being manipulated into feeling want the person would like you to feel and showing consideration for one's fee Manipulation is ruled by guilt, whereas consideration is ruled by love.

The process of making you feel responsible for another's emotions

Manipulators are sarcastic people. It's just their nature. They tend to spend a greater part of their time making a victim feel as if they cannot think on their own. On top of that, they tend to hold the other person responsible for all of their emotions.

When they are feeling sad, it's maybe becaue they experienced that as a victim of manipulation. When they become enraged, you should examine your actions to see if it has anything to do with you.

Manipulators have a tendency to take as much as they can from a victim while making them believe that they do not have the ability to take total control of their lives. On top of that, they enjoy making the victim feel unworthy. Manipulators love to ue certain phrases to coerce and blackmail the victim again and again by proving their love again and again. "If you truly loved me, you would have taken me to Paris" is a type of statement in which the manipulator uses emotion and guilt investment to propagate shame and guilt on the victim into doing something. No matter how innocent it may appear, it is still a type/form of maniplation.

They speak for, or about, you.

The manipulator manipulates the victim into advocating for him. When your partner stands up for you, it demonstrates loyalty and romance. However, it is a form of abuse when they speak over you or for you in public. They're acting as if you're incompetent and can't do it on your own.

They act as if the other person cannot do things on their own. As a result, if it's fnal date night, you might choose to enjoy your wine while the important other places your previously agreed upon orders. Manipulators tend to make their victims appear to have split personalities. When they're with family and friends, they'll be complaining about the partner, and in other situations, they'll be the ones defending the same individual they're complaining about.

The victim can vow to change her ways and hold the manipulator to lower expectations while also being agry with him for not meeting the expectations she held.

The victim believes she is unaware of or incapable of comprehending her personality. Her allegiances are constantly shifting. Her thoughts were jumbled and perplexing. The victim must understand that her version of herself that was aligned with him was not based on her original thoughts.

The Process of Closing and Withholding Emotional Intimacy

This manipulation technique has variou meanings. The term "motional withholding" refers to the process by which a partner evades or shuts down. nonverbally as a means of manipulating or exerting control over a situation This technique is painful for both parties involved and can be confusing for the person on the receiving end. Some of the advantages of being in a relationship include the ability to communicate your emotions with a partner, even when you are upset.

It is not advantaged for a partner to completely shut down without an explanation, leaving you in the dark trying to establish what you did to them. While everyone needs some personal space to process their feelings and thoughts, there are partners you will have to constantly beg to let you into their train of thoughts.

Convenient Neediness

Take a look at your partner; do they become weak or fall sick when things don't go their way? If you weren't aware, this is undeniably a form of manipulation, regardless of whether they're sick or not. Examples: If your partner refuses to have serious conversations, do they all of a sudden begin to feel faint?

Your partner is unwilling to go somewhere, and then you have to forfeit going because they want you to assist them with their anxiety, which ends all of a sudden when you decide to cancel your short trip. Your partner cannot help in the house mainly because they don't have the energy or experience. Many people are unaware that you can always arrange while your partner is being cared for.

Changing the object

While switching conversations may appear innocuous, it is a technique used by many manipulators to avoid accountability on many occasions. Many narcissists dislike being held accountable and will, as a result, intentionally create a diverge. If you choose to ignore it, this type of behaviour will continue for a long time making engage in any relevant or pressing issue difficult. You can always try "the broken record method" to fight back. Continue to point out all of the facts without succumbing to their dissatisfaction.

Redirect their redirection by saying things like that isn't exactly what I'm talking about. Can we stay focused on the real issue at hand? If they aren't interested, you can disengage and decide to spend your energy on something more constructive."

Speak first to establish a baseline, then search for weakness

A sizable percentage of people in the sales industry tend to do this to us all the time. They will be able to establish your baseline by asking us throbbing and general questions. They will also select your behaviour and thought patterns from which they will be able to evaluate your weaknesses and strengths. This manipulation tactic can also occurs in our workplaces and even in our relationships.

Deprivation

Another type of emotional manipulation is deprivation, which forces people to do things against their will. This type of manipulative behaviour is quite common in our social and familial lives. It's mainly used to coerce a person into compliance. Unlike other techniques, deprivation is extremely difficult to overcome. However, by being self-sufficient and having your source of income, you will be able to defeat this type of manipulative trap.

CHAPTER 5
Mind Control

What is mind control?

Mind control refers to the process by which an individual or a group uses unethical manipulative techniques to coerce other people to do what they want. Many times, it is in the favor of the person doing the manipulation. Mind control is also known as forced persuasion, thought reform, mental control, forced control, and brainwashing.

The term mind control has been used and applied to a variety of psychological techniques that can be expounded as taking another person's thoughts, emotions, decision making, and sense of control.

Many theories of mind control have been developed in the past to enlighten people on how authoritarian governments appear to be flourishing in indoctrinating captives. Torture techniques and propaganda ware used to control people's minds.

Most of these theories were later expanded and modified by psychologists. Ben Zablocki proposed the third-generation theory. It centred its efforts on the use of mind control to keep cult and NRM members.

The simplest way to understand mind control is to consider it as a structure of influences that greatly disrupts someone's beliefs, decision-making capabilities, relationships, behaviors, and needs.

Mind control is a subtle and pernicious process. It's subtle to imply that a person is unaware of the level of influence that is being imposed on him. Changes will be made by the victim as time passes. The victim believes he is making his own decisions. Not knowing that all decisions are being made for him. The process is insidious because its main purpose is to entrap and cause harm.

Mind control is a process because it does not happen instantly. It occurs over some time. The duration is influenced by factors such as the methods used, the experience and skill of the exploiter, and other social and personal factors.

The difference between Mind Control and Brainwashing

There are some intriguing distinctions to be made between brainwashing and mind control. For example, the target for this technique understands that the aggressor is the enemy in brainwashing. People who were captured during war are aware that the person doing the brainwashing is an enemy. The captives believe that changing their belief system is necessary for them to remain alive. They are tortured and forced to do things they would not normally do. However, when the captives escape, the brainwashing's influence disappears.

While mind control is more subtle and sophisticated. This is because a manipulator is typically a person known to the victim, so they are not genuinely attempting to defend themselves. In reality, she may be partaking willingly, believing that the manipulator has her best interests at heart. Torture is less dangerous than mind control. Although there is no physical coercion in mind control, it is far more effective in controlling a person. The reason being, brainwashing has the ability to change one's behavior, however, mind control will always the attitudes, thinking process and change beliefs, behavior

Victims of mind control have a difficult time accepting that someone they trusted has tricked and manipulated them. This is one of the main reasons why it is difficult to recognize mind control. The victim will not want to admit that they were manipulated without their knowledge.

Techniques of Mind Control

The techniques used to control others are a tantalizing form of destructive power. These tactics are are still used in various cultures. The mind processes diferent types of information, there are noticed, while others are overlooked. Regardless, the brain still processes these types of information.

What you may not realize is that our subconscious and conscious minds tend to filter this information at a faster rate.

Mind control techniques tend to influence a person's eventual actions mainly because they are the initial results of your mind's thoughts.

The methods uually ued are drawn from the Neuro-Linguistic Programming. The NLP has the ability to control one's mind with the assistance of well-equipped patterns and strategies.

Managing Thoughts

The laws of the mind are variou. These laws detail an effect and a cause. The mind's actions can be perceived externally. The G is capable of displaying the intensity of thought waves, the state of one's consciousness, alertness, and mental actions. Mental frequencies are known to be greater than the beta state in terms of mind frequencies bombarded by thought waves.

The alpha state is located next to the beta state. However, it has lower frequencies with lower thought waves where one's mind becomes quiet and calm. The alpha state happens to be an extremely mportant state in the world of psychology.

This is primarily because this is the state in which subconscious mind programming and hypnosis can take place. Classical hypnosis depends on the process used to put the subject into an alpha state so that their minds become more suggestive to commands and can be easily programmed.

While NLP techniques have the capability of inducing thoughts into a person's unconscious mind, these thoughts are consciously unnoticed. When it comes to neuro-linguistic programming, Persuasive power tends to be high because it's used in a variety of fields such as politics, marketing, and business.

While the level of frequencies of theta and alpha states and those of induced trance are similar, their attributes differ. lpha is the first step in meditation and will progress to higher levels as time goes on.

lpha is the initial state of meditation and will be progressed to a higher level with a modified state of consciousness.

Perception of Mind

The mind's perception of the environment sends intuitive signals as it influences people's thoughts.

Through mind perception, a person is likely to confuse or deceive another person's mind by passing the individual's conscious mind but likely to be picked by the subconscious mind.

Many mentalists' tricks tend to work under this principle. For example, a magician may wear a red tie, which the subject's unconscious minds will ignore. However, as the act progresses, the information is gradually fed into the subject's mind. It can be done by putting the word RD in the magician's monologue or other means that will automatically trigger the colour RD in the minds of the audience.

Thoughts can be induced in viewers in a methodical manner that manipulators use. The limitations of the mind happen to be beyond our perception. They can be easily programmed to undertake certain remarkable things.

Mind Control Types Peer Group Pressure and Social Proof Techniques

This technique entails supressing resistance and debt to new ideas thru the exploitation of one's need to belong People who want to manipulate large gatherings will employ the tactic of social proof.and peer pressure to mIND control the targets Social proof is a psychological phenomenon in and of itself. It basically means people assuming that the beliefs and actions and believes other people are appropriate because they can see that This tactic works best when a person is unsure of how to behave, what to do, or what to think. Many people in such situations will observe what other people are doing and do the same.

Hypnosis

Hypnosis, which is frequently associated with sideshow performers, is a fairly common technique that is not a magical act as many people believe.

Instead, it's a technique that's used to put someone in a state of increased concentration, where they're more open to suggestions. Many people disguise this state as meditation or relaxation to induce it.

A therapeutic technique is hypnosis. The suggestions are conveyed to people who have undergoned a procedure designed to help them relax and be able to focus their minds. Therapists tend to ue hypnosis to aid patients in breaking free from bad habits, such as smoking, or achieving other positive changes. They accomplish this with the assistance of soothing verbal repetition and mental imagery, which leads the patient into a half-conscious state. The patients' minds will be more open to reconstructive messages once they have relaxed.

There are numerous methods for hypnotizing someone.

- The state of the room - The state of a room is essential in the process of hypnotizing victims. It necessitates special lighting; fluorescent lights happen to be the best because they are not very dim, but also not extremely harsh. The temperature of the room also plays a role in the process. It should be a little cooler than usual. normal room temperature The victim must remain unaware and relaxed.
- Music played in the background must be receptive – the music should be a beat that is somewhat similar to the beats of the human heart, ranging from 45 to 72 beats. Especially during study sessions, as the music will help you concentrate and relax better.

Roll the Voice — The term "voice roll" refers to a patterned, paced style used by hypnotists when influencing a trance. When they are keen on entrenching a point in the juror's mind, a number of lawyer's majority of who happen to be extremely good hypnotists ue voice rolls. The voice roll may sound as if the speaker is speaking to a metronome beat. Alternatively, it can sound as if they were emphasizing each word in a patterned and monotonous style. To maximize the effect, the words will be delivered at a rate of 45 to 60 beats per minute.

The voice call technique can also be ued in churches. The pastor will begin the service by establishing the process. He will then induce a reshaped level of consciousness by generating expectations and excitement among the congregation. This will be followed by a group of women dressed in pure and sweet dresses. The ladies will appear, followed by a song. The gospel songs are uually great for rangement and excitement.

As the song progresses, one of the women may be "smitten by the Spirit" and fall or act as if influenced by a spiritual force. This tends to effectively make the atmosphere more intense within the church. Conversion tactics and hypnosis are being used together at this time. The result? The audience's attention will be focused on the communication, while the surrounding environment will become more intense and exciting.

Humans remain completely awake during the hypnotic process. Statistics show that the average person will enter a hypnotic state.state at least twice every day wthout ever noticing There are many applications for hypnosis, such as relieving pain, blocking memories, breaking bad habits, and treating autism. However, not every **person can succumb to hypnosis.**

Imaginary events may create sadness, real fear, or happiness, and one may even be traumatized in her seat if he is surprised by someon Researchers classify daydreams as a type of self-hypnosis.

Milton Erickson, a pioneer in hypnosis, demonstrated that people tend to hypnotize themselves on a day to basis. However, many psychiatrists tend to focu on a daydream state attached through focusing exercises and intentional relaxation. This type of deep hypnosis is frequently compared to the relaxed state of the mind between sleep and wakefulness.

Once in conventional hypnosis, the unsuspected victim will approach the hypnotist's suggestions or ideas as if they were his own and a reality. When you are in such a state, you are also very unwittingly embrace it completely. This is the primary reason why many stage hypnotist shows are entertaining. If the person performing the hypnosis suggests that one of your legs be swollen up almost twice its size, you will feel a sensation within your leg and may have difficulty walking.

If the hypnotist suggests that you drink hot coffee, you will be able to taste it as well as feel its warmth in your throat and mouth. If the hypnotist decides to suggest that you are either afraid or in danger, you may feel shaky and sweaty. However, the entire time, you will be aware that everything I all imaginary.

People will feel relaxed and uninhibited in this state. Because they can tune out the doubts and worries that tend to keep their actions in check. You may have experience a similar feeling when watching movies As you become more engrossed in the plot, you begin to worry about your friends, job, and family, among other things. are going to vanish until all you can think about is what's on the screen.

Adults will suddenly begin walking all over the stage barking like dogs or alternatively sing as loud as the can during hypnotists' shows, casually sensible and reserved. The fear of being embarrassed will cease to exist. The person's sense of morality and safety will remain established throughout their experiences. The hypnotist can't make you do anything you don't want to do.

Subliminal Programming

This is the process by which the mind controller creates an anchor within a target, making it simple to place the victim in any given state simply by touching or tapping and sublimely programming the victim's mind. Subliminal reference reference reference reference reference reference reference reference reference reference reference reference They can either be presented to the subject as an audio suggestion, visual suggestions that are airbrushed, brilliantly included in the design of an image or picture, hidden behind this subliminal programming technique often comes in tapes that offer oral proposals recorded at extremely low frequencies or volume. The oldest audio subliminal technique employs the ue of a voice which follows music's volume so subliminally making it quite difficult to detect without the ue of a parametric equalizer. However, this practice happens to be patented, and thus when a person is keen on developing their own line of audio cassettes infused with subliminal, they are required to negoti Sound engineers have discovered a way to alter and fuse suggestions so that they are projected in a similar frequency and chord as the music. This, in turn, has the effect of making you feel like you're a part of the song or music. However, they discovered later that by using such a technique, there was no way of reducing different frequencies so that the subliminal can be detected Regardless, the suggestions are still being heard by one's subconscious mind. The messages cannot be monitored even with the most sophisticated equipment.

The book series by Bryan Key on the use of subliminal in political campaigns and advertising well documents the abuse and misuse in different areas, specially in printed advertising such as magazines.

However, the big qestion about subliminal message is: does subliminal message work? It has been proven that the subliminal works. Subliminal suggestions behind various department stores may be instructing the cutomers not to shoplift. An investigation was carried out in a department store on the ast Coast. The store reported a 37 per cent reduction in thefts after 9 months of testing.

Paying attention to the Person

This technique entails paying attention to different cues of an individual's such as body breathing pattern, gestures, pupil dilation, eye movements, body language, and anxiety. The specialists are able to deduce one's state of mind by associating an instant emotion with a person's bodily cues. The movements of one's eyes can be acknowledged to establish how one perceives and processes information.

If a victim is asked about the colour of their house and they replied by moving their eyes to the top right corner of their eyes, then the answer is created visually. If she moves her eyes to the left-top corner, it will be classified as visual remembrance because she is attempting to remember the colour of the house.

Effective way of ung hot words

NLP (Neuro-Linguistic Programming) professionals tend to ue specific patterns of words that may seem normal but always laxer and more indicative. These hot words tend to be more connected wth the senses and are more sugestive. Words like see, hear this, finally, feel free, means, and because may make an impression. try to invoke a specific state of mind, such as feeling, imagining, and experience. It also creates the desired perception in one's mind. Programmers also tend to ue specific vague words to control one's thoughts.

Repetition

This technique entails repetition that is constantly being made. It's a tool for controlling persuasion. This tactic may appear too simple to be considered effective; however, repeating the same message over and over makes it easier and more familiar to remember. When this technique is combined with some social proof, the desired message is delivered without failure.

The existence of affirmations is another event that repetition works. If you can persuade yourself through consistent repetition, there is a chance that someone will try and employ repetition while trying to control you into behaving and thinking in a certain way.

Techniques of Mind Control

Persuasion technique is another manipulation technique of the human mind, whereby the manipulated party is aware of what caused his/her opinion shift. The main basis of persuasion is to try and access an individual's right brain. The brain's left half tends to be rational and analytical. The right half is creative and imaginative.

The idea of persuasion is to distort one's left brain side and keep it busy. The persuader will generate an eye-opening modified state of consciousness, causing the shift from Beta state awareness to lpha in a victim.

This type of activity carried out by the brain of a shift can be measured ung a G machine. Politicians ue these techniques in daily lives, gatherings, or during campaigns, but lawyers ue it in many variations and are known as tightening the noose.

During a politician's speech, the politican may generate what is known as a yes set. The yes set are basically statements made by the politican to cause the listeners to agree. The listeners may even unknowingly nod their heads in agreement. The truisms come after this act. Truisms are basically facts that can be debated; however, once a politician has the target audience agreeing, the odds are always in the favor of politicians because the audience will stop thinking Finally, there is a suggestion. The suggestions will entail what the politician will want you to execute or do, and becaue you have been in agreement all along, you may be easily persuaded to agree with the suggestions.

An example of a politian's speech

Are you fed up with high food prices, ladies and gentlemen? Are you fed up with astronomical gas prices? Are you fed up with out-of-control inflation? Well, you know that the other party allowed 20 percent inflation last year; you know robbery has increased 45 percent nationwide in the last 12 months; and you know your paycheck hardly covers your Well, the resolution to these problems is to elect me, Dwayne Wilson, to the congress."

This technique also includes mbedded Commands. As an example: The speaker will make a gesture with their left hand on certain keywords. According to research, gestures from the left hand are more apt to have direct access to the right brain. The media-oriented spellbinders and politicians tend to be carefully trained by a team of experienced specialists who tend to use every trick in their books to manipulate

Neuro-Linguistics techniques and concepts are heavily protected. Individuals who are willing to devote their time and money to the program can receive neuro-Linguistic training. Some of the most subtle and powerful manipulations are found in persuasion technique. It also describes a manipulation tactic known as an intersperse technique, and the idea behind this technique is to mention one thing with words at the same time plant a subliminal impression of another thing in the minds of viewers and listeners

Vibrato

Vibrato refers to the tremulous effect that's imparted in numerous instrumental and vocal music, using a cycle-per-second range that causes people to go in an alter

At one point in English history, all singers whose voices included pronounced vibrato could not perform publicly because the listeners would end up having fantasies and going into an altered state, which was often sexual. People who attend opera or enjoy familiar music to it are affected by a altered state induced by performers.

Isolation

This technique entails inducing reality loss through physical separation from friends, family, rational references, and society. Isolation of physical nature tends to be extremely powerful, but even if physical isolation is not practical or impossible, the manipulators will try to segregate you mentally.

This can be achieved in several ways, ranging from attending two weeks of seminars in another country to condemning your family members, friends, and colleagues. The ultimate goal is to limit any form of influence by controlling the flow of information.

Advertise and propaganda

This mind-controlling technique employs mass media. These media forms are designed to reach as many people as they can. Mast media include movies, television, radio, magazines, daily newspapers, video games, records, and the internet.

A number of researches have been carried out in the past decades to try and measure the effects of mass media on the general population. These were done to come up with the best techniques to try and influence it. The field research research research research r Communication science was developed and is now used in public relations, marketing, and politics. Mass communication is an important tool for ensuring the functionality of democracy.

Edward Bernays was the founter of the consumerist culture, which was designed to target people's self-image primarily to turn them went into a need. Initially, this was envisioned for specific products such as cigarettes. However, in his 1928 book, Propaganda, Bernays also stated that "propaganda" happens to be the executive arm of the useable government." We can see this most clearly in the current police state and the ever-growing snitch culture, wrapped up with the pseudo-patriotic fight on Terror. The ever-increasing consolidation of media has authorized the entire existing corporate structure to consolidate with the government, which now employs the ideology of propaganda placement. Media; television, print, cable news, and movie can now seamlessly work to merge an overall message that may seem to have a ring of truth mainly becaus When one becomes accustomed to identifying the main "message," one will be able to see this type of imprinting everywhere, including subliminal messaging.

Sleep Deprivation and Fatigue

This mind-controlling tactic is attained by creating vulnerability and disorientation by prolonging physical and mental activity and withholding adequate sleep and rest. s fatigue and lack of sleep lead to a person being mentally and physically tired Someone who is physically tired and less alert tends to be less alert and more susceptible to persuasion. According to research mentioned in the Journal of xperimental Psychology, individuals who had not yet slept in the last 21 hours are normally more susceptible and open to suggestions.

Methods of Mind Control

It is possible to teach the mind not to be controlled by others. There are numerou ways people in society can achieve this.

I. Believe in yourself and your ability to change.

Someone who wants to be mentally strong must believe. If a victim does not believe that they can change, then they will not try as hard as they can if they believe that they can. As a result, they must ensure that they are using positive thinking to deal with their problems. Keeping in mind that they can change the way they think hence they can improve. Various studies have shown that people who adopt a "growth" mindset are more likely to make continuous improvements than those who see their skills and traits as unchangeable and fixed.

II. Be confident in your abilities.

Many people believe that being accurate about their ability to control themselves is crucial. Regardless, studies show that if you are more optimistic about your ability to take full control of your behaviour, you will be able to achieve more self-control.

To become optimistic, try and tell your inner self that you are going to succeed and gain full control of your mind, over and over, whether you believe it or not.

Also, try to remind yourself of times when you were able to successfully control your breath and mind as intended. You should reflect on your successes rather than any self-control failures you may have experienced.

III. Cease overgeneralizing

Overgeneralizing simply refers to the process of taking one occurrence of a negative experience and then projecting the experience onto other experiences or to your predictions People must seize this opportunity to shape their future through consistent perseverance and hard work. For example, someone who had a difficult childhood and believes that their life will be difficult in the future challenger, need to may ways he wants her life to improve, and work to improve them. Those who want a more meaningful relationship or a better job may need to conduct research on the various methods of obtaining these things. The individual should then set goals for himself in the various domains to accomplish.

IV. Do not jump to conclusions.

This tactic is a thought trap that entails thinking certain things without having any kind of evidence to back them up. A person who tends to jump to conclusions may believe that another person despises him or her without having any evidence to back up this claim. For one to jump to conclusions, they can employ different ways, such as pausing and thinking more before reaching any judgments. It can assist you in asking yourself questions about the thought. And individual can ask himself if he really knows that the thought he have is true or false. He can also ask himself to identifiy detailed pieces of evidence that would suggest that the thought I true. Someone who believes a person does not like him/her may have to ask themselves to identify specific conversations with the individual in order to provide evidence for their claims.

V. avert catastrophizing

Catastrophizing is simply defined as a pessimistic thought trap in which the person tends to exaggerate scenarios or situations. person catastrophizing after failing an exam may utter statements like "My life is ruined." I'm never going to get a good job. To avoid catastrophizing, the person must work on processing things in a positive manner. He can also ask himself questions that require reasoning and logic. People who have just failed a test and believe that their lives are ruined because they will never get a good job may ask themselves, "Do I know anyone who has failed a test yet still gotten a good job and/or seems to?" "Would I make my entire decision based on that person's grade in a single class if I was hiring someone?"

VI. Make obstacles for yourself

The best way to control the mind is to make it more difficult for the mind to obtain what it requires. You should starve it occasionally. The additional effort will enable this part of the mind, which is less likely to win and influence one's behavior. When one keeps clicking on the snooze button early in the morning, he can place the phone far from the bed. This will compel the individual to get out of bed to turn it off. Another mode is when you want to control the part of your mind that wants to watch TV when you're not watching it. If you want to cut down on TV watching time, you could place your remote control in a difficult-to-reach location.

VII. Pray for your sucessful self-control efforts.

This technique is really helpful as a type of motivation. When you manage to successfully control your mind, you should reward yourself to encourage yourself to continue doing so in the later dates. For example, if you do not feel like doing laundry and cleaning the house but managed to force yourself to do the test anyway, then you should reward yourself with your favorite pastime However, be careful not to make the reward/gift too excessive, or you may find yourself beyond control and then back to where you started. If your main goal is to be able to study and you managed to force the mind and managed to do the studying when you actually never felt like doing, then don't treat yourself too much or you might just end up losing the progress you made.

VIII. Punish unsuccessful self-control efforts.

While we strive for good behaviour and success, it's also important to punish yourself for any lapses in self-control. As a matter of fact, Studies show that the threat of punishment forces the mind to embrace self-control.

To ensure that the punishment was effective, ensure that it was placed in the mind of another person, either a close friend, partner, or family member. You could ask them to ask your dessert as an example. If you fail to gain the established self-control measures by the end of the day, they will withhold the dessert.

Mind Control Applications

Mind control has a variety of applications. It has beneficial ways of ue.

Propel forward - Once you have complete control of your mind, it will be easy for you to move forward in your file. The influence you will have will be much greater and more useful in your life. This will only work if your intentions aren't selfish or negative by nature.

Most therapists will agree that hypnosis is an effective and powerful therapeutic technique that can be used to address a wide range of conditions such as mood disorders, Hypnosis is widely used to help people change their habits, such as binge drinking or smoking.

Hypnosis helps people cope with a variety of negative emotional states such as anxiety and stress, fatigue, mood disorders, insomnias, and mood disorders.

Creating one's tickets -You can use mind control to get other people to do things for you. If you gain control over someone, you will definitely be able to make certain things work for you.

Completing larger sums-While we tend to believe that a lot of hands will always make light work. Thus, putting many hands to work will be more easy for work that would have been difficult to accomplish alone. Even if the person feels as if they have been given an advantage, they will be pleased that they were able to accomplish something that you needed assistance with.

This type of gratification and satisfaction will always make these individuals overlook that they were controlled.

Manipulation of circumstance- Having positive control over one's mind means being able to manipulate certain situations with ease. Two hands always better than one, and when you have someone that you can depend on in your corner, then you are going to be able to manipulate the circumstances and situation

Intimidating the opposition- The most powerful armies are known for their massive numbers. Having a mind under your control will always give you a soldier who will help you stand firm in any battle. When needed, these soldiers will take fire. While this is not always the moral and ethical path to take, it will always come in handy, especially when dealing with difficult situations.

Regardless, certain people tend to ue mind control techniques unethically. Basic mind control techniques are widely used by sects and cults to indoctrinate, recruit, and retain members. Many of the leaders of these sects and cults are psychopaths.

According to Robert Hare, a psychology expert, many psychopaths employ these techniques to begin a relationship with another person so they can control and dominate them. These mind control techniques ideas can be applied to one on one relationships. Narcissists are another group that regularly ues these tools.

CHAPTER 6
Mastering Your Emotions

What exactly is an emotion? Motion is a person's personality that consists of their feelings rather than their thoughts. Conscious intellectual reaction such as happiness or sadness is experienced as a strong feeling often directed toward a specific object and typically accompanied by physiological and biological.

Motion is a determining factor that influences how we live and interact with others. Most people believe that their emotions rule over humans. There are many different types of emotions. They affect the choices people make, the actions taken, and the perceptions we have are all affected by the feelings we are experience. Some of the basic emotions felt include:

Fear

Fear is typically a response to impending danger. Fear is a survival mechanism in the animal kingdom. It could be a mild caution or extreme paranoia. Fear is a strong emotion that can play an important role in survival. Someone who is in danger or experiencing anxiety goes through flight response. The muscles tense, the heart rate and respiration increase, and the mind becomes more alert, priming the person's body to either run from the danger or stand and fight. This fear reaction helps to ensure that one is prepared to deal with threats in his surroundings effectively.

A person experiencing fear's body language can include:

- facial expressions such as broadening the eyes
- forts to flee from the danger and help threats
- Breathing heavy and rapidly

Heartbeat rate increaes

People react to fear in various ways. Most people are more sensitive to worry, and specific situations or objects are more likely to trigger the fear. Some people, on the other hand, may develop a more similar reaction to the anticipated threats or even the thoughts about the potential dangers. This act is believed to be anxiety. Anxiety about social situations is referred to as social anxiety. Others may look for fear-inducing positions. Extreme sports and various other thrills may be fear-inducing, but for some people, it may seem to thrive and even tend to enjoy such feelings.

The act of being repeatedly exposed to a fear situation may lead to acclimatation and familiarity, which may reduce feelings of anxiety and fear. It is the main behance behance behance behance behance behance behance behance. This technique is used by therapists to gradually expose their patients to the things that frighten them in a safe and controlled manner. Finally, fear feelings may begin to decrease.

Surprise

The surprise is ordinarily quite brief and is ordinarily distinguished by a physiological surprise response after something unexpected. Shock can be positive, negative, or neutral. A great example of a pleasant surprise would be arriving at your workplace only to discover that your coworkers have gathered to celebrate your birthday.

The body language of someone surprised entails:
- Yelling, breathless, or shouting are examples of verbal reactions.
- facial expressions such as opening the mouth or widening the eyes,

- Physical responses such as jumping back

This type of emotion can easily trigger a flight response. Surprised people may be subjected to a burst of adrenaline, which helps prepare one's body to either flee or fight. This type of emotion may have an impact on human behaviour. For example, studies have shown that individuals tend to notice unexpected events.

Suspiciously. It is the main reason why, in the news, unusual and extraordinary games will always stand out in memory in comparasion to others. Studies have also discovered that people are typically more swayed by unexpected and unexpected arguments.

Disgust

The body language expressed during this type of emotion entails:
- Facial gestures such as curling the upper lip
- The folding of the nose
- Turning away
- The body reacts physically as well, such as vomiting or retching.

Disgust can be caused by a variety of factors, including an unpleasant sight, taste, or smell. Disgust is a normal reaction experienced when people taste or smell foods that are rotten or gone bad. Infection, poor hygiene, rot, death, and blood may alo trigger a similar response. People may also be subjected to moral disgust when they see other people engaging in behaviours that they consider immoral, evil, or distasteful.

Happiness
This emotion is the one that motivates people to strive for success. Happiness may be defined as a pleasant emotional state characterized by feelings of joy, content, satisfaction, gratification, and well-being. Since the 1950s, the number of happiness researches have dramatically researches have dramatically researches have dramatically researc Positive psychology, a branch of psychology, has researched the state of happiness.

Happiness can often be expressed through:

- relaxed body language
- facial expressions such as laughing, playfulness, and smiling
- An upbeat and pleasant tone

While joy is one of the basic human emotions, the things we believe will lead to happiness are heavily influenced by culture. The realities of what exactly contributes to happiness tend to be more individualized and complex. Studies have come out to support the idea that happiness and health are connect. It demonstrates that happiness can have an impact on both mental and physical health. Happiness has been linked to a variety of outcomes, including increased longevity and increased marital satisfaction. Unhappy people are more likely to have a variety of poor health outcomes. Stress, anxiety, and depression have been linked to a number of things such as decreased immunity, decreased life expectancy and increased inflammation.

How to Master Your Movements

"Anyone may become angry, and that is easy. However, to be angry with the right person at the right time, and for the right purpose and in the right way – that is not within everyone's power.

Mastering your emotions will necessitate a degree of awareness, which not everyone intends to have. Understand various emotional languages and become acquainted with their flaws. Once you've figured out how to effectively express your emotions, you'll be a lot better at understanding them.

There are numerous ways someone can learn to master emotions and help himselfself, not let emotions dictate behavior.

Cultivate Emotional Intelligence

Different images may be suggested by emotional intelligence. It simply refers to the process of getting your brain to create the most useful instance of the essential emotional concepts in any given situation. This act will requere you to adjust your concepts: rather than piling all similar emotions under one universal term. You can try to learn more about the nuanced meanings of a variety of emotions like misery, which may come in a variety of flavors such as enragement, bitterness, mortification, and irritability There are a number of ways to make you feel great, such as being thrilled, ecstatic, and grateful.

From the moment you wake up each morning, you have the option of either enjoying the day, being fully engaged in your life, or being motivated. The best way to break the cycle of negative emotions is to adopt a more positive attitude. Actively looking for new ways to adapt to negative moods will help us repair our spirit and also improve our responses and overall thinking. Emotions are the foundations of who we are, as well as an untapped source of potential for our survival. We all can experience negative and positive emotions, and learn how to regulate these feelings to come up with the best response, which is the key to our emotional in

Knowing more about the ability to differentiate between the subtle nuances of different emotions will make you an emotion specialist and also assist your brain by giving you more options to forecast and categorize differen It will also assist you in better tailoring your actions to your environment.

Learn to SAY NO

It entails people who have codependency problems. Most people with codependency symptoms struggle with saying NO and sticking to it. They may be able to say NO a couple of times, perhaps once or twice, but they eventually give in. People in sales enjoy working with people who have this symptom. It's because they know they can get them to buy what they're selling at a price that gives them a fat commission.

Codependents affect personal relationships because they become a pushover. One is controlled in an emotional state where his/her needs are usually ignored. You believe you are a caring partner, but you are jeopardizing the relationship. This is because you aren't honest with yourself or your partner.

One must learn to say no in the business world. Learning to say no is one of the most powerful negotiating tools in the business.

Gather New Experiences

Instead of repeating the same old patterns and behaviors, let go of the past and begin accumulating new experiences. Be an experience collector. Unique experiences that you acquire through reading books, learning about other cultures, going on trips and adventures, watching movies, acquiring new perspectives, trying fresh foods, lear Doing all of these things will help you shift your perspective and also what you expect will happen next. Acquiring new skills helps encourage your brain to create new concepts and bind the old ones in new ways. As a result, affecting future behaviour and predictions. By putting yourself in the shoes of others, you will be able to develop and strengthen your compassion muscle. For example, expanding your vocabulary may lead to improved emotional health by offering new concepts. This, in turn, will not only help you become better equipped to deal with a variety of circumstances, but it will also improve your negotiation skills and increase your empathy.

Recognize Negative Thought Patterns

People's behaviours are usually a response to emotions, and these emotions are usually a response to one's thoughts. Most people are aware of what cognitive behavioural therapy is known as cognitive distortions. It can be explained further as someone filtering out experiences to demonstrate some point about their core beliefs. If one feels unworthy of unconditional love, or if one has destined a life filled with misery, the person will progress by accumulating evidence to support that. We tend to catastrophize minor issues, personalizing things that have nothing to do with us and, as a result, limiting our potential. This is where the majority of these rampant thoughts may be helpful. We should understand if our thought patterns are resultant of correct facts or just assumptions that we make.

Negative emotions may be suffocated as a result. Continue by distinguishing your emotions more precisely. Learning to identify different emotions with greater granularity will help us regulate our emotions more effectively.

This is since emotions provide individuals with more information on how to regulate their behavior as well as how to deal with various circumstances. Individuals who are able to separate ideally between the emotions had a less chance of resorting to feeling overwhelmed especially under stress, according to research. Another study found that individuals who fear snakes labeled their emotions using different fear and anxiety words. They became les anxious when they were around snakes. However, when 6th and 5th graders decided to enrich their vocabulary with emotion words, they were able to perform more better in class and improve their social behavior when in school. On the other hand, people with depressive disorders and social anxiety tend to portray and experience fewer negative emotions in their day to day.

Do Your Own Thing and Take Charge of It?
Someone who has hate coming his/her way is very good at determining who the hate is coming from and the credibility of the said information. If he/she get revenge from someone who isn't even close to her/his level, it won't affect him/her at all. When getting hate from someone level or above, then he is likely to take a closer look at it. It is because when someone who is on your level or better criticizes you. It can be used to make adjustments. You should consider it an opportunity for me to improve.

Someone who is speaking out of hate and jealousy is likely to be beneath you. So, when the happen, you know that if you get a lot of hate for doing what you love, that mean you are doing the right thing! Take charge of it. However, if you were receiving criticism from those above you, use that criticism to make adjustments and see where you can improve. It is for this reason that people looking for relationships should always try to date someone compatible with them.

Working hard like them, moving forward, and love getting better. Any criticism you receive from this person will be critical, and you will not take it lightly. It can aid you in bettering yourself and growing.

Find the good in every situation and appreciate your feelings.
You need to ask yourself tough questions like, "What else could this mean? What is good about this?" Forcing yourself to find the good in each and every situation will assist you to alter how you truly feel about it. It is critical at this exact stage that you do not resist the emotion you will experience. Thus, it is therefore important that you acknowledge

openly the feeling that you are currently experiencing and also search for the true meaning and importance in the situation

Portraying resistance will only lead to uncertainty and will also prevent you from conventing this emotion into something you can use and work with as you progress. The concepts will be entrenched and reinforced within our universe model whenever we decide to direct our attention to. Attending and savoring and positive thoughts will make them easier to notice, thereby assisting you to predict and come up with future scenarios of positivity.

For example, if something unexpectedly made you feel disgusted. Instead of fighting, hiding, or attempting to resist the disgust, you should recognize the feeling of disgust and that certain circumstances have unexpectedly triggered this emotion. When you can recognize this emotion, you will be ready to progress.

Two diferent people may have similar experiences but react differently. For example, two people may join the military. During a tour, each of the two soldiers will lose a hand. One person immediately begins to associate this event with their life being over.

I'll be the same as before. No one will ever love me again. I feel depressed." he becomes suicidal and ends up killing himself. The other person, who also lost a hand in the event, however, finds a true and empowering meaning behind the event. I'm grateful that I still have my other leg. I'm so grateful that I still have my arms, hands, head, and other parts of my body." The person ends up being appreciative and portrays gratitude.

Strip Your Feelings to the Bone

An individual needs to do somatic work on his/her emotions. Somatic work means that you begin to understand how feelings live within the body rather than how the feelings control the mind. It can be an excellent tool for mastering them.

It allows us to work on our flaws while also developing in different areas of our lives where we tend to struggle emotionally.

Use peaceful imagery. When we are not careful, various strong emotions may send our mind pacing out of control. We may begin to picture and image all the negative outcomes.

Technique Deep Breathing

People tend to use deep breathing to calm their bodies and ensure that they do not get worked up. However, in cases where painful feelings emerge, begin by closing your eyes and then picturing a calming image. You should then breathe slowly a calming feeling and

If it's a negative thought and you find it quite distressing, then work to readjust your thoughts in a positive manner. Put more fun and leiure into your day to

Learn to distinguish your emotions more precisely.

One of the most important things you can do at this stage is to become curious. Curiosity will open doors to new opportunities and perspectives, allowing us to gain distinct insights into our emotions as well as the situations we may find ourselves in.

If you're curious about the emotions you'll be experiencing, you should ask yourself;

What is the true worth of an emotion?
What must I invest to make things much better? In what ways does this emotion/emotion serve me?
What do I feel and desire?
Try to figure out the circumstances that make you feel jealous, scared, and angry.

In many people's lives, they frequently feel angry when they are being ignored, unappreciated, or disrespected. Thus, if you ask a person numerous times to do something and then some per

During this period, remember that irrespective of the emotion that you will be experiencing, it is normally there to influence all of your actions. It has various uses such as to teach you

Nonetheless, you must be willing to seek the necessary answers that will assist you in gaining crucial insights that are needed to overcome many of the emotional roadblocks that you

Learning how to distinguish emotions with improved granularity will help people regulate their feelings better mainly because it offers them more information concerning how to regulate their behavior and

Deconstruct and categorize your feelings.
It's important to learn how to break down a feeling into mere physical sensations, rather than letting these sensations become a filter that you choose to view the world from.

Many people have displayed improved test performance and public speaking after establishing and recategorizing anxiety as a part of the body's natural coping

Separation of physical sensations can help individuals who suffer from chronic pain crave fewer pain killers and view depression as a physical sensation rather than a personal catastrophe.

"When you feel bad, treat yourself like you have a virus, rather than assuming that your unpleasant feelings mean somether personal." "Your feelings may be raucous,"

How to Acquire Grander Self-wareness
It's critical to feel all of your emotions physically. What changes within your body will you ignore? You might notice an increase in your heart rate, tensions within your muscles, or a tumble in your stomach.

Becoming aware of certain cues is a great place to begin identifying your emotions. Forther, you should recognize what are some of the things that trigger your emotions.

To acknowledge the triggers and cues, keep a journal for all your emotions throughout the day. Pen down the emotions that you emote will experience throughout the day; <u>who were you spending your time with, what exactly were you doing</u>, and how was the atmosphere, was it intense?

Writing is more visceral and tied to your feelings than typing, so this is one time you should go old school and write down your thoughts. Be consistent, do a daily habit is best. Start small with just a few minutes each morning while you still have control over your time.

A great way to remember these positive experiences is to pent them down. On top of that, contemplating the expected adverse effects will make it much easier

Write whatever comes to mind, without filtering your thoughts or emotions. Consider a trigger question if it helps stimulate your thinking. Keep the journal to yourself. You may choose to act on the insights you gain from your journaling, but your raw, written thoughts and emotions are for you only.

Always pay close attention every time you feel that you are under stress. Highly sensitive times are a great situation to get feedback for your triggers, symptoms, and cues of emotional stress.

When you are talking negatively, a partner can help you point out when you are falling back to destructive patterns.

Keep Your Body Maintaine

Energy, emotions, and mood tend to be affected greatly by the type of food that we eat. Regulating our diets, nightly sleep, and daily exercises can help us make outstand are keen on balanced stated and working through certain emotions.

Maintaining a balanced body budget and getting enough sleep are some of the advantage we here regularly.

The simplest way to manage one's emotions at any given time is to move one's body. For example, animals tend to get their balance back by making long movements. A simple and unplanned movement will reduce neural activity within one's submit

On top of that, the basics of sleep, exercise, nutrition, and a healthy body can be achieved through a number of other means, which may include spending time outdoors, enjoying nature

On the other hand, meditation gives us the chance of practicing our ability to observe and then experience emotions without any judgment.

Have a good 'People Filter.'

Socially, you don't want to be so easy to let people into your life. Having a sound filtering system will come through experience. The more you're around people, the more you'll know who and who even writing a blog, whatever, ue this time to be productive. There' nothing wrong with someone being single and moving/herself forward.

Cultivate Awe

We refer to the feeling which inhabits within the pleasure's upper reaches and just on the boundary of fear. It can significantly boost our body budgets in different ways.

Wonder has been found to arouse curiosity, interconnectedness, and a desire to explore. Nature offers numerous occasions to experience awe.

Awe tends to evoke a sweeping presence of grandness, from the falling snow from a mountain peak to the turbulence of an ocean to the faultless rainbow.

Forgiveness and Drop Grudges

This rule is fundamental for someone to manage his or her emotions. One must learn the art of letting go of the past and forgiving those who have offended you. If he or she does not let go of these deep feelings, it will only lead to further harm.

It's not an easy process, and you may have to remind yourself to do it for a while until you're free of it.

Don't Allow Others to Control Your Emotional Status

This rule applies to everybody that has those pesky, negative friends and family that always tend to bring you down. The reason why this rule plays a vital role in our lives is that words do matter

It's easy for people to tell you not to listen to your critics, but I don't recommend it because the only time criticism affects you is when it comes from those who matter to you, even if it's only for a few minutes.

The fact that you get affected by other people is because you probably care about these people. If you're dating someone who consistently brings you down, it makes perfect sense that those words hurt you.

When you focus on the big picture, it's much easier to ignore the hate that comes your way. If you're dating someone with abandonment issues, these hateful words are from a much deeper, inner fear that's projected onto you.

Gain Confidence in Your Ability to Handle Motion
In this stage, ensure that you go through the first step of the IQ matrix. Under the IQ matrix, people learn the true meaning of all the 10 critical emotional steps and then

On top of that, it's the ideal time to achieve some certainty and also carefully select the emotional response that you intend to experience.
and knowledge that you may need to handle your response effectively.

To nail this situation, recall a time or period in your past where you managed this emotion effectively and then used the emotion to your benefit. The memory that you will use will act as

Don't try to fit in; instead, be inspired but not dependent.
The modern society is a very captivating one. People have access to loads of information and at a click. The world has become a global village. There's nothing wrong with this. You should see this an opportunity to connect

It becomes a problem when, instead of being self-sufficient and growing on your own, you begin to shift the responsibility of growth to someone else.

Take Some Space for a While

It's necessary to make space for a few days, even few weeks or months from the situation and person you'll be reacting too negatively.

Do not anyone about your problems.

How many institutions have you informed that their actions made you angry or in a certain way?

Following fact or reality, it's clear that other people's actions and words affect us in one way or another.

While this is the case, we must also accept responsibility for the various emotions that we will experience as a result of the actions or words. Furthermore, no person can make you feel anything; it is always a choice to read.

Creating a Trustworthy Financial Relationship Amongst Couples

The society believes that love is the foundation of a sucessful marriage. In the U.S., money issues are the third leading causes of divorces after infidelity and repuls

Money issues, if not addressed, can ruin sucessful marriages. For the marriage to work, couples need financial discipline and stability.

Some financial ideas that can help build a strong, sucessful relationship with your significant other are listed below.

When should you open a joint or separate savings account?

Marriage is a partnership between two different people, so opening a joint account is an effient way to watch.

On the other hand, operating a joint account makes financing simpler and motivates team spirit in couples. Couples that get married in their late years are allowed to operate separa accustomed to financial freedom, though they are advied to have a joint account for expenses accrued during the time of marriage.

Creating a Budget

Having a budget has many advantages within a household. Roughly 32 per cent of people in the US operate using a budget. It helps track money spending and also plan

Belief Is Key

The moment a spouse stashes away money in a different account, it creates financial animosity, which reduces trust.

Debt Transparency

Couples need to be transparent with each other in terms of debts. It's important to let your partner know the amount of debt that you're into. If possible, consult them before taking a loan.

Financial infidelity aries when a spouse keeps secret purchases or credit card from their partner. Having debt secrets can make you insecure, hence

Consider hiring a financial advisor

Money issues can sometimes get out of hand, and frequent disagreements about money can breed animosity between couples.

Couples can seek the aid of a financial planner, which relives the partners because a third party will not be motivated by self-interests.

Set Realistic Goals

Some marriage problems arise when couples have too much expectation and it is not met. Maybe, some financial goals that were set were too ambitious. Expectations should be minimized, and the goals should also be realistic.

Empowering Your Employees Using Role-playing in E-Learning

Role-playing in training situations can be an effient way of realizing a team of competent and well-trained employees for any company.

Why is role-playing training required for employees?
The benefits of role-playing training are numerou. The organization facilitating the training and the employees on the receiving end have a lot to gain from role-playing.

- Developing accountable and problem-solving abilities in employees
- Employees become intuitive in dealing with real-life problems at work.
- The trainees' listening skills are sharpened.
- Trainees can improve their decision-making abilities.
- Teamwork for the employees ha been enhanced
- The trainees gain confidence in their ability to handle real-life work situations because role-playing training simulates real-life situations.
- Institutions can learn the fundamental characteristics and evaluate the work ethics of their employees.

Role-playing forms in training
Role-playing can take various forms depending on the number of employees being trained and the organization. The type of role-play training an organization decides to use has simila

Playing a Single Role
In this situation, the organization divides the trainees into different groups, and one group is chosen to perform the demonstrations of the given task while the rest of the group(s) makes observations. The groups then analyze the exhibit and share the lessons learned.

Many role-players
The trainees are divided into groups in multiple role-playing training. All the groups of trainees demonstrate the various situations the organization gives them simultaneously for role-playing, the

Role-Playing on the Spot
Spontaneous role-playing has one trainee playing the role of an actual trainee while the other trainee's playout tasks that the actual trainee is

Rotational Role-Playing

In this role play, the groups of trainees demonstrate a skill. for the demonstration of one ability, the trainer takes over and sets up a discussion of the presentation

With the advancement in technology in this era, all forms of role-playing training can be effectively assimilately assimilated to training programs in organizations by creating plat-learning role-play training outperforms traditional training because trainers and trainers find it more immersive and engaging.

Master of motival master of motiva

Most sportsmen believe that their emotional state is permanent and that they have very little control over their emotions. The same people believe

They also have unproductive and unhealthy emotional habits, which affect their ability to achieve goals and perform well. thletes can gain control of their emotions. They need to do away with the lousy perception and believe they are masters of their minds and thoughts

Despite being a simple choice, emotions are a sophisticated choice at any given moment. It's important to note that emotions are not a natural choice. will arise and select a positive emotional response, leading to successful execution and great feelings

Mastery of motival mastery

What emotional mastery means for you to recognize the adverse psychological reactions which affect your performances. Whenever you start to experience negative emotions during a competition.

After identifying the stimuli that affect us, we should begin examining our beliefs and programs. What are some of the things that cause us to act in the manner that we do when a stimulus enters our minds?

We will want to discover what we believe in, what makes the stimulus unacceptable or threatening to us.

What is it in our values system that is causing us to react so harshly? The emotions can be frustration, anger, and despair, and you need to detect what triggers these situations.

Considering what the cause leading to the situation is going to entail a careful examination of your emotional baggage., If your emotions are too strong, you are going to find a therapist.

Their guidance can enable you to better understand your emotional habits, and the therapist can help you to learn new emotional responses that will better serve.

If you want to keen the emotional master process, then specify different emotional reacts to situations that usually trigger these negative emotions. ncouraging emotional responses will assist you to overcome any past mistakes or wrongdoing. It acts as a motivating factor that influences your performance, produces positive emotions, which will, in turn,this positive reaction will not come naturally at first because your negative emotional habits are deeply ingrained.

However, they also need to ensure that they stay focused on feeling better. Their performance will always improve.

You must believe that you can do it, that you can deal with the emotion right away. The easiest, quickest, and most potent way of dealing with a feeling is to recall an occasion in your past when you experienced a similar emotion.

You should then acknowledge that you had handled the situation successfully before. If you managed to deal with the situation in the past, it is more than possible to deal with it again.

Consider all the ways you can be able to deal with emotions throughout history and then use this as a blueprint for what you can do at the moment to alter the way you can be feeling.

Do things in the same way you did before, believing that they will work the same way they did before. For example, if you are feeling lonely, then you can look back in the past when you experienced the same feeling and as

Did you react by calling your friends and then stayed in touch with them after the call? Did you plan a visit to your friend's house? Whatever you did in the past, you should try it once more and chances are you will get similar results.

Develop Curiosity for the Message that the movement offers You

Enabling one's curiosity will help us manage our emotions, prevent similar problems from recurring, and solve various challenges.

Some of the questions you can ask yourself when confronted with negative emotions are:

- How do I feel?
- What does this imply?
- What lesson can I get out of this?

You are in command, so accept responsibility for your actions.

Many people dislike taking responsibility for their actions, particularly those who have difficulty controlling their emotions. Those who suffer from anger issues have a difficult time accepting responsibility for their wrath because it is usually external stimuli.

Our feelings come from our thoughts, and our thoughts are usually based on our belief systems. It isn't always easy to pinpoint the exact emotion that one is experiencing, and it's also important not to put an end to surface emotions like hatred, jealousy, or anger.

These superficial emotions will result from a number of deeper emotions based on the feelings of lake of acceptance, weakness, and fear.

People do not feel angry unless they are afraid of losing something important to them, such as a relationship or property. Anger is always accompanied by fear, hurt, inability, disappointments, and being alone.

We should also examine positive emotions to understand what we believe will make us happy when we receive a specific stimulus. This will aid us in understanding the beliefs that make us unhappy when we do not receive the stimulus. emotions and then try to assess and dissolve the emotional mechanisms experienced, which create anger so that we can be able to create substantial happiness, love

Recognize that your Reaction is not in line with your Values.
When an individual has the feeling of being miserable, it's many times because they are experiencing an unpleasant effect resulting from physical sensations. The individual's brain will try to pre

The more concepts you know and scenarios you can create, the more effective you will be in regulating your behavior and managing your emotions.

This type of recategorization can quickly results in noticeable benefits.

People who recategorize anxiety as some sort of excitement have fewer symptoms of stress, especially when addressing the public or during the interview through the sympathetic nervous system.

However, with fewer proinflammatory cytokes, people feel terrible and lower performance, they perform better.

Anger and emotional mechanisms analysis have yielded a lot of understanding, mostly on how we react that result from our

We tend to react in accordance with how we feel. On top of that, we tend to feel in accordance with how we are pre-programmed to think. The stimulus will pass through our beliefs, in turn, creating feelings and finally warranting the

Some people may channel their negative energy into self-rejection, overeating, anxiety, or depression.

In most scenarios, those who are angry may try to forcefully change people around them and anyone they may be in contact with a number of ways to ensure that the world and

People will always feel intimidated when efforts to change their programming tries to happen. We would feel the same way if someone wanted to change ours.

Meditate

Meditation refers to the practice of intensive focus on a sound, visualization, movement, attention itself to increase the apprehension of the present moment, reduce stress, promote

In many organizations, the best way to achieve something is to do nothing.

Though this statement may appear to be controversial, on this occasion, simply 'being' is more than enough to transform our mood. nanyone can perform a quick meditation at any given time, especially when the person needs to calm down and

Close your eyes and focus on breathing; repeat this process until you are able to calm down. Feel the exhale and inhale, and remember to count your breaths.

Do whatever it takes to keep your focus on your breathing and away from the situation at hand. The timeout will enable someone to gather thoughts and perhaps see the situation from a different angle.

People can decide how they respond to different situations. Between the response given and the stimuli lies our ability to act freely; the freedom of selecting how exactly you may want

People can think and decide independently while overlooking conditioned reflexes.

How will you be able to make the real choices? To make the real choices, you must first understand what to expect and want from your behaviour.

One must be efficient and respectful in their communication while at work.

It's also important to recognize that you might experience negative emotions such as frustration and anger because of the brain's fast-acting right side.

Your ideal response should always be positive, something that will help you achieve results towards a respectful workplace. always take the high road when presented with such issues.

Before xecution, planning

To control your emotional dealings with a process is to define the process clearly, a well-developed trading plan should create a trading environment where n efficient trading plan should cover the current market environment, the entry and exit processes, and multiple scenarios that could invalidate a setup or an ex

Having a plan also reduces the anxiety you have as a trader. as mentioned earlier, this plan disconnects you from the process to some level because you can

People'S Deal with Negative Motion

People have different ways of mastering their emotions when confronted with either positive or negative emotions. Below are some of the ways one can deal with negative emotions.

- voidance- voidance simply refers to the avoidance of all types of situations that have the potential of resulting in negative emotions. which we tend to avoid taking risks. another great example of avoidance is the avoidance of approaching strangers because we want to avoid failure or rejection.
- Denial- Denial entails dissociating oneself from negative emotions by coming up with reasons that try to explain why things happened the way they did. However, with this approach, ignoring the message tends to only worsen until you pay att
- Competition- Involves the ue of negative emotions as a way to become unique and make it part of your identity; you tend to ue negative emotions to undermine or overlook other people's problem

Learning and Using

ventually, you will want to learn more from your negative emotions and then find methods of ung them. Mastering your emotions I the the first step to understanding that all fee

When you change your understanding of negative emotions to signify something more, action Signals, then your beliefs will become your coach, mentor, and ally. Feelings will become a guideline, support system

Action signals will notify you that whatever you are doing at the time may not be working.

You will only experience negative emotions as a result of the procedures you will ue or perceiving certain things.

As mentioned earlier when discussing the Motional Triad, perceptions refer to the way we interpret certain things and we can alter our attitude by asking better qestions and changing our psychology.

It's critical to remember that we are the source of our emotions, and thus we are the ones who create them.

At any given moment, you can decide how you want to feel. Remember that you don't need a specific reason to be in a great mood.

CHAPTER 7
The Art of Subliminal Messages

Subliminal message can be defined as an auditory or visual message that is presented fast or slow to target only those who pay attention. Many researchers have examined the effect of subliminal messages as a way of passing information to the correct audience. What has become clear is that subliminal messages have an impact on how an audience perceives certain crucial details in product advertisement. When utlized correctly, it can result in an increase in overall sales of the items offered by different companies.

Merkle and Cheeseman came up with the Psychodynamic ctivation in 1986. A theory that suggests how subliminal messages work on different people. The theory proposes that subliminal messages instigate an unconscious defence mechanism in the individual who sees or hears the message. It then places the individual in the position of desiring to satisfy two complementary features as portrayed in the subliminal messages. As a result, they end up purchasing a product that they would not have purchased in the absence of the subliminal messages. This unconscious stimulus is what leads to the positive impact of subliminal messages as a persuasion tool.

Many companies have used subliminal messages to advertise their products over the years. A common example is a phrase "Drink Coffee and Eat Popcorn," which was popular in the mid-1990s. This increased product pair sales, especially after watching movies at different theatres. Subliminal messages are made to affect an individual's actions proactively without them realizng any new changes. the messages are everywhere; be it the gym, the movie shop, or the bookstores. Companies use subliminal messages to get their target audience to stop doing certain things in favour of their products.

So, does subliminal messaging produce results, or are the facts misrepresented? Some researchers, such as Greenwald and Spangenberg, have given subliminal messages a thumbs up as a way of convincing a population mass to think in a certain direction. As a result, it causes an increase in the sales of the items that a certain manufacturer offers. But you have to be wise when connecting the subliminal messages. The phrases should not be overly obvious. Instead, they should demonstrate a co-relationship between two independent activities. Subliminal messages have The majority of them are emotionally attached to the messages portrayed by the subliminal cards.

Brief History of Subliminal Messages

The first-ever recorded book about subliminal messages was called "The New Psychology," and it was published by Scripture in 1907. The book described the basics and principles of subliminal messages. That's a clear indication that the art 0of subliminal messages have been art 0f messages have been art 0of messages have been art 0of messages ha Another early recorded example of subliminal messages is by Knight Dunlap, a merican psychology professor. Knight created an illusion of Muller-Lyre in his presentation by including two pointed arrows of varying lengths. These arrows subliminally influenced his subjects based on the length of the shadow lines. Since then, researchers have carried out various visual subliminal experiments to carrie a workable theory.

The visual flash technique has also been ued in various fields. One such example was when soldiers in World War II were trained on how to identify a plane in 1/100th of a second. Pictues of various planes were passed on the display board, and each soldier was expected to name that plane. This technique was used to enable soldiers to quickly identify enemy planes and shoot them down as quickly as possible.

James Vicar carried out research on the impact of visual display of subliminal messages in 1957. During a movie presentation at the New Jersey theatre, James ued a tachistoscope and projected

"Drink Coca-Cola" and "Hungry?" "At popcorn." He did this for 1/3000 of a second after every five seconds during the movie reenactment. This saw an increase in Coca-Cola and Popcorn sales to an all-time high of 58 percent. This caught the attention of the business world, and soon, every corporate was looking for unique ways of writing subliminal messages to the target audience.

In 1979, about fifty stores in Canada and the U.S. started broadcasting messages about shoplifting in audiotapes. During this era, most stores suffered losses as a result of shoplifting scenarios. Incorporating subliminal messages with soothing background music was a good start. The stores saved about $600,000 because store theft was reduced by 37 percent. The auditory background messages had a Since then, many stores around the world have implemented this technique to reduce store theft and promote new products.

Subliminal messages in music have been linked to anti-social behaviour. Some musicians don't always pay attention to what they're writing. When they talk about sex, guns, and other forms of violence, their fans get motivated to do what they hear on the records. This calls for the responsibility of musicians and other relevant governing bodies tasked with the responsibility of inspecting any released content. The subliminal messages portrayed in such records also have an impact on the relationship between musicians and fans. When their favorite artist sidelines them to hate another artist, mot fan chooe to chooe to chooe to chooe to chooe to chooe

Subliminal messages are powerful persuasion tools, as recent years have revealed. More people are embracing this art to increase sales and control a target audience in a particular direction. In addition, researchers are still making wonderful strides in this field, and we can only expect new innovations soon. The beauty of subliminal messaging is that it targets a series of events that have have have have have have have have have have have have have

On the other hand, it enables business owners to accurately record the effects that arise as a result of its impact.

Subliminal Message TYPES

There are two types of subliminal messages: auditory subliminal messages and visual subliminal messages. These messages are nearly identical, but their impact is felt differently. They also have diferent results in terms of effectiveness and workability. However, instances of visual subliminal messages have been around for the longest term. Auditory subliminal messages evolved from visual counterparts. However, there is no doubt that their effect cannot be understimated. When used together, they produce exemplary results that a single persuasion tool cannot. Here's what you need to know about these two types of subliminal messages.

Subliminal Messages Visual

Multiple studies have shown that visual subliminal messages stimulate people's cognition. As such, it enables them to identify with specific items. However, these subliminal messages must be projected to the audience on a regular and consistent basis before being sucessful. Hormones govern how our bodies function. When people see something that excites them, they will go the extra mile to find a solution. That is why the visual subliminal messages should be writen creatively to spark interest in the target audience.

Visual subliminal messages often aim at messing around with the target audience's self-esteem. Many people feel belittled when someone speaks on anything that touches their ego or convenience. As a result, the visual subliminal messages frequently give suggestions of complementary pairs that you should focus on. However, the messages have to be derect and polite. Avoid using excessively provocative words when creating visual subliminal messages. This will put you in a target audience backlash which is bad for business. So, do extensive research on the theme at hand before making any persuasion advances.

Visual subliminal messages have played a The once-simple tool has transitioned to become a very powerful marketing jewel to the global business community. Such acts are common everywhere, as they have been incorporated in almost every aspect of our lives. On the other hand, researchers are always looking for new ways to make this marketing technique better. With the strides that have been made in the industry, we can only expect more inventions in this field shortly. The use of visual subliminal messages has grown even more in social media. The available platforms give business owners a large audience in one shot.

Auditory Subliminal Messages

The auditory subliminal messages are meant to drive specific information embedded in background music or any other debate. This marketing technique is a subset of visual subliminal messages. However, most researcher have discovered that the two are effective when ued together. Initially, business owners focused solely on advertising via visual subliminal messages. They frequently did this because they believed that incorporating audio messages would result in backlash from those who want to enjoy their beautiful time. However, this technique has now evolved to be one of the best marketing tools especially in supermarkets and other large retail shops.

Sometimes you want to reach a large audience by speaking to every single person at once. However, doing so may necessitate large sums of money being invested in roadshow campaigns and other advertisement schemes that attract large masses. This menace can be solved by embedding subliminal messages in your audience's favorite music or radio station programs. People will likely listen to those over whom they have a great deal of responsibility. On the other hand, it is common for people to filter what they want to hear in different situations.

Auditory subliminal messages are common in the entertainment industry. Nowadays, big artists are paid to mention brand names in their songs, interviews, or shows. Some artists have even signed on as brand ambassadors, allowing them to promote companies in a variety of settings. The world of advertisement is slowly recognizing the importance of auditory subliminal messages for better sales and company growth. This marketing technique is undeniably excellent, especially when targeting a non-repulsive target. Most start-ups are gradually incorporating this marketer to join the league of sucessful business owners. We can only expect more ideas to develop in this beautiful marketing field with current world innovations.

After sending subliminal messages to the audience, the ball is now in their court. Different people perceive messages in different ways. Some may accept the message, while others may choose to ignore it. However, when a subliminal message is effiently drafted, the reach out should be huged. So, what do you do to ensure that your message interpreted? Or, what are the ways of ensuring that your subliminal messages feature detailed information in one shot?

Subliminal messages, on the other hand, can be harsh if they are not well-crafted. The target audience may feel as if you are taking advantage of their situation by manipulating them to buy your products. Such scenarios can be avoided by conducting research on the audience's needs. To woo a particular audience, you should identify the people and use relevant subliminal messages. Only write or record what is necessary for the audience. For example, when promoting your gym services, ensure that you only emphasize the drop-in training prices and how you have excellent training partners. Don't tell the audience what they shouldn't eat if they haven't yet joined your gym.

When administering subliminal messages, you should be prepared for worst-case scenarios. Don't expect everything to go as planned. Instead, plan how you'll counter-attack any negatives feedback. A good counter-attack should be the one that provides permanent solutions to the problem at hand. You can only find such a solution if you involve an expert. Always consult with successful business brands to gain more insight into subliminal messaging. Benchmarking allows you to learn more about subliminal messages as well as what you should avoid if you want to be successful in your persuasion efforts.

Conclusion

Manipulative predators frequently shift their blames to other people. They frequently want to make their victims feel as if they had a hand in their misfortune. As a result, if you fall into such traps, you'll be vulnerable to manipulation tactics by devious predators. The majority of them do not want to be corrected and always imply that everything should revolve around them. The result is that their ideologies are spread to unsuspecting victims. Their negative thoughts should not have an impact on how you go about your daily activities.

Manipulative predators capitalize on transferring their misfortune to other victims. They do not wish to be alone in their unfortunate circumstances. As a result, they work tirelessly to ensure that a few victims are included in their misfortune. If you soften your stance against their cunning behaviors, you'll likely get integrated into their sinister moves. You'll only find out when it's too late, and the repercussions are far too severe to handle. That will be a success in the manipulators' advances. Their manipulation tactics have already had an impact on the lives of unsuspecting victims.

Most psychopaths and narcists make extensive use of this technique. They typically target unsuspecting victims and shift the blame so that they do not feel alone in their mess. A quick way to combat this is to focus solely on the positives. Don't let someone ruin your day because they had a bad adventure. Such negativity can have an impact on how you conduct your daily business. It also reduces your morale when dealing with certain life problems. You should be in a good mood to conquer your day-to-day adventures. Manipulative predators, on the other hand, aren't happy when they see that everything in your life is going swimmingly. They will thus devise evil motives to ensure that they gain control of your mood and twitch it to favour their ill motives.

Be brave enough to face your problems head-on. Don't let manipulative predator's prawn on your ideologies and persuade you otherwise. Also, stand firm in your decisions. Most manipulators notice when you are divided when making important decisions. They will thus try to talk you out to ensure that you change your perception.

On the other hand, they'll try to conjure up a negative image of what you believe is workable in your situation.

The war against emotional freedom is not for the faint of heart. It necessitates dedication and commitment. Always consider the benefits you'll receive if you stick to your principles. Don't get too caught up in what the manipulators will think of you. Remember that most manipulators do not have your best interests at heart. They simply want to ensure that you 'worship' their traits. Their goal is to staunch unsuspecting victims into becoming 'believers' of their selfish principles. As a result, be smart and focu on what pleaes your soul. It's a long journey, but with persistence and dedication, nothing is impossible. So, be strong and concentrate on the end goal of emotional freedom.